THE LIFE AND ART OF
W. HEATH ROBINSON

Photograph by RONALD PROCTER

W. HEATH ROBINSON

THE LIFE AND ART

OF

W. HEATH ROBINSON

by

LANGSTON DAY

LONDON
HERBERT JOSEPH LIMITED

FIRST PUBLISHED IN NOVEMBER, 1947

PRINTED IN GREAT BRITAIN BY
ODHAMS (WATFORD) LTD., WATFORD, HERTS

CONTENTS

LIST OF ILLUSTRATIONS

ACKNOWLEDGMENTS

I AM particularly grateful to Mr. T. H. Robinson who has given me a great deal of information about his brother's early life; also to Mrs. Heath Robinson and her family for written facts and patience under questioning; to Mr. Ernest Huson, Mr. J. M. Evans, and to Mr. John Gledhill who has allowed some of the original pictures by Heath Robinson which are in his possession to be reproduced.

My sincere thanks also to the following for their spoken or written contributions: Mr. Reginald Arkell, Mr. O. M. Badcock, Mr. Ernest Boot, Dr. Liliane Clopet, Mr. Ian Coster, Mr. F. C. Dickinson, Mr. P. B. Hickling, Mr. Cecil Hunt, Mr. S. Jacobs, Mr. William Latey, Mr. John Napper, Mr. Bertram Prance, Mr. Frank Reynolds, Mr. G. L. Stampa, Mr. John Stirling, Mr. Frank Swinnerton, Mr. Bert Thomas, Mr. Guy Worsdell, and to Messrs. Blackie and Son for permision to quote from *My Line of Life*.

INTRODUCTION

SIXTY-FIVE years ago machinery was still regarded as the deity of a new religion and many of its worshippers had the intolerance of a fanatical priesthood. Who could doubt that mankind was on a steeply ascending slope? Had not a host of scientific thinkers—Mendelev, Faraday, Clerk-Maxwell, Darwin, Müller, Comte—explained the mysteries which had baffled the human race since the days of Adam? Could there be any end to scientific progress? Mechanical inventors of genius were as plentiful as peas, and at last the toolmakers and the machine manufacturers had caught up with them.

Machines were pouring out of the engineering factories, marvels of construction were proving how far we had soared above the heads of preceding generations. Iron bridges, iron ships, iron buildings showed the superiority of modern man to his primitive ancestors who worked in wood. The Firth of Forth Bridge had been started in 1869. The iron-built *City of Chester* was crossing the Atlantic in just over eight days. The Crystal Palace stood like a mighty hot-house forcing the growth of fresh mechanical marvels.

In the " Sooty Seventies " the clouds which issued from the factory chimneys were the smoke from plutocratic Britain's cigar, the vulgar and visible sign of success. Benjamin Franklin's eccentric suggestion that the unburnt carbon should be used a second time as fuel was scoffed at. Was not the Machine a beneficent deity whose caprices should not be questioned, even if he blackened the lungs of his worshippers?

Moreover, for his greater glory he was about to undergo a metamorphosis. Faraday, Volta, Ohm, Ampère, Glavani, Oërsted and others had been preparing the ground for an even more splendid generation of machines. Before the end of the century there was to appear the magneto and the internal combustion engine, the electric motor, the dynamo, electric lighting, the telegraph and the telephone. Many people believed that humanity was becoming almost a race of demi-gods with sovereign power over the forces of nature and full knowledge of how to settle all their social problems. The words of Dr. Ure, the panegyrist of industrialism, were still quoted with complacency. His unctuous dicta were a part of our industrial liturgy.

" This island," he wrote, " is pre-eminent among civilized nations for the prodigious development of its factory wealth, and has been therefore long viewed with a jealous admiration by foreign powers. . . . The blessings which physico-mechanical science has bestowed on society, and the means it has still in store for ameliorating the lot of mankind, have been too little dwelt upon. . . . The constant aim and effect of scientific improvement in manufactures are philanthropic. . . . At every step of each manufacturing process described in this volume the humanity of science will be manifest. . . . The present is distinguished from every preceding age by an universal ardour of enterprise in arts and manufactures. Nationals, convinced at length that war is always a losing game, have converted their swords and muskets into factory implements. . . ."*

Moving in a mysterious way its wonders to perform, the Machine was believed to solve its own problems as it went along, and distribute blessings even if at first sight they did not appear as such. The sacred law of

* The Philosophy of Manufacture, by Andrew Ure.

supply and demand regulated the flow of production automatically, and if anyone did not get enough goods it was surely because he was lazy, feckless, or improvident. On the other hand, if factory owners amassed huge fortunes it proved that they possessed the Christian virtues, even if they employed sweated labour. And if they made money by supplying cheap liquor or adulterated food, this did not detract from their moral worth, because the economics of Adam Smith had superseded the Laws of Moses.

An extraordinary harshness and pomposity had entered into human ideals, and even the utopias had undergone a startling change. Some of these ideal cities were built entirely of iron. Utopian States were organized on Fascist lines, and some of them were like the most hideous dreams of Mr. H. G. Wells.

In earlier days Man was considered a bird of passage bound for an eternal kingdom, but gradually this picture of him had changed to that of a creature who would build a Kingdom of Heaven on earth, served by millions of mechanical slaves. In this new religion of the Machine, eternity was replaced by time, and salvation by the conquest of nature. At the same time Man was thought to be progressing, in time, far more rapidly than ever before. The prophetic visions of Erasmus Darwin and Old Mother Shipton were being fulfilled at last. People were travelling faster and faster. Great locomotives were roaring across England through towns which a short time before were served only by antiquated horse coaches.

" Let the great world spin for ever down the ringing grooves of change," Tennyson intoned, on seeing one of these monsters.

Such a public idol had the Machine become that the scientists discovered that the universe was itself a machine, in which the stars in their courses were moving like the balls of a governor and the Milky Way was some gigantic crankshaft. The Creator, of course, was a master mechanic who in the tradition of modern mechanical invention had designed this great piece of apparatus and had even wound it up one fine morning in the remote past. One day it would run down and the human race would perish. But this was a long way off, and in the meantime mankind had become a master race—for had it not learned to create machines like its Creator?

The more mechanized life became, the more closely it approached creation. Progress, in fact, could be measured by the extent to which manual operations were taken over by machines. The skilled handicrafts were merging into the mists of a primitive past upon which a modern man could look back with easy scorn. For a man of the seventies, progress led to some Wellsian utopia in which everything would be performed by machines and all values would be measured in terms of financial profit.

Of course, this extreme view was not held by everyone, nor was it so clearly formulated even by the fanatics. But such ideas were sufficiently popular to provoke a strong reaction among men who valued human happiness more than economic abstractions and human lives above horse-power. They saw clearly that the Machine was becoming a Frankenstein monster. William Blake had been horrified by the " dark Satanic mills." Spengler looked forward to a time when machines would be destroyed and forgotten like the lost cities of Yucatan. Samuel Butler imagined a country in which inventors of machinery would be put to death.

Southey was almost in despair. Writing of mechanical industry, he said : " It is a wen, a fungous excrescence from the body politic; the growth might have been checked, if the consequences had been apprehended in time; but now it has acquired so great a bulk, its nerves have branched so widely, and the vessels of the tumour are so inosculated into some of the principal veins and arteries of the natural system, that to remove it by absorption is impossible, and excision would be fatal."

Men like Southey revolted against machinery because they saw that the financio-industrial world was built on a new system of thought which looked at things " in the flat "; a system which left out all the intangibles, which are really the most important and the most real. Nothing was now considered real unless it could be weighed, measured, or counted. Time was real, so men's lives were regulated strictly by the clock; and there arose a new breed of missionaries, like Baxter, whose creed was work. Money was supremely real, so everything must be subordinated to financial profit. As for Man, he was dehumanized into an economic unit, a mere cog in the Machine, whose business was to serve the new deity and whose private feelings scarcely came into the reckoning.

I think it was St. Augustine who defined sin as the substitution of means for ends. Certainly it was Kant who said that human beings should be treated as ends, not as means. This was just what the new industrialism did not do. Men were expected to give up a life of freedom and adventure and follow a mechanical routine. They went to work to earn the bread to gain the strength to go to work to earn the bread. . . . And their taskmasters bought bigger machines to win greater fortunes to buy bigger machines to win greater fortunes. . . . The Machine had begun to make Man in its own image.

In some of the mediæval utopias, such as Roger Bacon's, the Machine was to come as Man's deliverer, but in fact it came as a tyrant, an abstract counterfeit of the universe, existing for its own ends and dragging humanity captive behind its triumphal car. Merrie England was replaced by a land of solemn utilitarianism. Iron and soot pervaded the landscape and coated the country with a sombre veneer of grey or black. Men wore black clothes, black boots, black hats resembling their factory chimneys. They drove in black carriages and blackened the air with coal which they burned in black hearths. The central shrine of the deity was called the Black Country. If a man escaped by death from this dingy paradise his widow had to go in black for three years. Was this general sabotage of colour a sign of depression and foreboding?

None of the earlier enthusiasts doubted that machines would enable men to get more out of life, but actually nothing is more remarkable than the contrast between the triumph of means and the poverty of the ends. In the seventies great rotary presses, marvels of human ingenuity, were pouring out printed matter—as they do today—much of which was near the level of imbecility. Sixty years later Mr. Stuart Chase, in America, pointed out the glaring disparity between the technical wonders of a broadcasting station and the inanity of the vapid political blurb which it disseminates.

Economics also underwent a change for the worse. In the nineteenth century, missionaries of the new Church Militant risked their lives to discover native tribes onto whom boots, bowler hats and bicycles might be thrust, if necessary by force. At home the first armies of modern salesmen were going forth to educate the British public in the habits of buying machine-made goods for which they had no natural desire. The old idea of satisfying natural needs had given way to a system of creating an artificial demand and then satisfying it only in part so that prices could be kept high.

Craftsmanship began to disappear. A generation of

machine worshippers arose who used machines to perform functions which could be done just as well, or better, by hand. Methods of manufacture were said to be " efficient " if they could turn out a spate of goods fit for marketing in bulk. A glance at some of the old advertisements shows what a torrent of useless mass-produced goods were being foisted on the public. Many of the dubious medical remedies and futile apparatus for increasing the strength would make present-day readers smile. But after six years of intensive use of the Machine for destruction, we cannot afford to smile too broadly.

It was evident to many that worship of the Machine was a dangerous new religion and that though it might make a useful servant, mechanical invention made a very bad master. Artists and writers were heretics, and so on the whole was the Catholic Church. The working classes feared and mistrusted it. They smashed Papin's steam boat and Arkwright's frames. When some of Bessemer's first sheets of metal broke, the workers broke into loud cheers! The protest against the Machine took other forms also. One of them was a cult of the past, an escapist movement which tried to revive old art forms, local languages and regional costumes. Another was a back-to-nature movement which aimed at putting the clock back and which took as its ideal the sort of life led by Robinson Crusoe.

All these direct antagonisms were bound to fail because history is irreversible. It is never possible to return to previous conditions, for when once the potentialities of some inherent situation have been worked out, the mould is destroyed and a new mould takes its place from which a further series of events streams forth.

The idea of the Machine is one such mould, and for better or worse its possibilities must be unfolded in history. Attempts to smash the machine were useless, direct verbal attacks on mechanization were certain to fail, not only because machines are mere instruments, neither good nor evil in themselves, but because direct attacks usually create equally great resistances which cancel them out.

Some indirect and subtle form of criticism was needed, some means of undermining our pious attitude towards machinery and showing that our undue reverence for the false god was ridiculous. Blasphemous laughter must break out in the temple of industry. The levers and the cranks, the gears and the flywheels, the winches, the belts and the pulleys, so revered by Victorian industrialists must be divested of their sanctity, and the bald, solemn men who served these deified monsters must learn to laugh at themselves and their priestly rites. Everyone must be made to see that a process, just because it was carried out by mechanical means, was not *ipso facto* sacrosanct, nor even necessarily sensible. Though the means might be a lasting monument to the ingenuity of man, the ends could well be insignificant, or even ludicrous.

Such ideas could best be conveyed visually. The situation, in fact, called for an inspired caricaturist who could persuade the worshippers of the Machine to laugh at their own idol.

As I hope to show in this biography, Heath Robinson, the first and perhaps the last true caricaturist of machinery, did precisely this, and the fact that he had no deep purpose in mind but only a desire to amuse his public did not lessen his power as a " debunker " of machine worship. On the contrary, by avoiding any attempt to moralize, he produced a subtle and lasting effect which no sermonizer could possibly have achieved.

CHAPTER I

INNKEEPERS AND ARTISTS

WILLIAM HEATH ROBINSON, who was born on May 31, 1872, in Hornsey Rise, North London, came of men who were jovial innkeepers, seafarers and adventurers, artists and craftsmen. He described himself as almost a Cockney because he was born nearly within the sound of Bow Bells. If a Cockney is a man with a taste for the bizarre, witty, observant and good humoured, he was wholly one.

The patriarch of the family, Thomas Robinson, began life as a bookbinder in his birthplace of Newcastle-on-Tyne, where he bound books for Thomas Bewick, the wood engraver. Bewick was the first man who successfully combined the professions of wood engraver and artist; he engraved his own designs and showed the true possibilities of the wood block. Perhaps Thomas Robinson bound some of those classic illustrated books of Bewick's such as *British Birds* and *British Quadrupeds*. If so he played some part in a most interesting movement, for under Bewick's influence wood engraving became something more than a mechanical routine. After a time some of the newspapers woke up to the beauties of the new technique, and both *The Observer* and *The Times* began to publish engravings.

Thomas Robinson bound books for George Stephenson, father of the steam locomotive, whom he knew personally. This was in the days when industrialism was gaining momentum and the self-centralizing forces of Finance were drawing the rural populations into the big towns. Grandfather Thomas felt the pull, and packing up his few belongings he worked his passage to London in a collier.

Here he gave up bookbinding for the more exciting business of wood engraving. He engraved for Fred Walker, who was drawing for *Punch's* famous offshoot, *Once a Week*; for Sir John Gilbert and J. E. Millais, in that popular illustrated shilling magazine, *London Society*; for du Maurier and for Charles Keene. A sketch of him by his grandson shows a bearded figure with long, untidy hair, poring over a wood block with an eyeshade and a magnifying glass.

In those days wood engravers, who were commonly known as " peckers," worked by day and often by night, sitting at a round table with a gas-lamp in the centre. The lamp was surrounded by a circle of big glass globes filled with water to focus the light on to the blocks, which rested upon little leather bags, or sand-filled cushions. Many wood engravers were deaf and dumb, and were known as " dummies."

Engraving in the Bewick tradition was an exacting task, calling for a good deal of patience and skill as well as the soul of an artist. Grandfather Thomas possessed all these qualities. He also had a strong family instinct, and for many years his home in North London was the headquarters of the Robinson clan. At his great Christmas parties every branch of the family met together under his roof.

His passage in a collier from Newcastle was a sign of something else which stirred in the Robinson soul: a love of adventure. This was expressed more strongly in his brother, Great-Uncle Matthew, who was drowned at sea before his great-nephews were old enough to know him. Heath Robinson said there was romance in the very thought of him. He and his brothers pictured him as an almost mythical figure, his arms tattooed with strange devices, and always willing to oblige with a racy tale of adventure or a nautical catch. With a whimsical twist he described his sad end. It seems that Great-Uncle Matthew was one day sleeping in the fore-chains of his ship when a bucketful of cold water was thrown over him by a well-meaning shipmate. Such was the shock that he sprang up, lost his balance and fell into the sea; nor was he ever seen again. This tragic tale saddened the boys, but, he said: " We rather enjoyed being saddened."

The genial side of our artist owed something to Grandfather William Heath who kept three or four inns at different times round about the (in those days) rural districts of Hammersmith, Uxbridge, Hounslow, Southall and Shepherd's Bush. The names of some of them sound a little strange today. He kept the " Red Cow " in the Hammersmith Road, the " British Queen " at Shepherd's Bush, the " Queen Adelaide " in the Uxbridge Road, and an inn called the " Pack-horse and Talbot "—the " talbot " being the dog which accompanied the packhorse on its travels.

Heath Robinson's mother used to describe the old inns as she remembered them in her childhood. She would watch the coachmen in their heavy green great-coats and grey top-hats warming their hands before the huge kitchen fire and their stomachs with hot grog, while the passengers stamped their feet and stretched their cramped limbs, making the most of the few minutes while their teams were changed. The yard outside rang with the clippety-clop of horses' hooves and the shouts of ostlers. Ragged little Irish urchins would come and beg for crusts, or impudently tender a doctored penny for a twopenny bit.

William Heath was in some ways a true Boniface,

bluff, jovial, too free with his hospitality for his own good. Three times he made a fortune and three times he lost it. Once he kept a country inn near a military depot and in his easygoing way he allowed the officers to run up large bills. The outbreak of the Crimean War called them away suddenly and many of the bills remained unpaid. He was forced to close his inn. Perhaps he had not the true temperament for an innkeeper because he was said to know Latin and Greek, and even to have written a play. Whether this was an exaggeration of some small learning in the days when many could neither read nor write it is hard to say, but on his daughter's marriage certificate he proudly signed himself " William Heath, Yeoman."

His broad and generous life spent in inns and taverns among coachmen, carters and travellers, and lapped by the boisterous tides of the high road, must have given his grandson, Will, something of that charitable attitude towards the world which was always so evident in his life and work. And from his grandmother, Thomas Robinson's wife, came some of the well-known Heath Robinson wit. This lady handed on her sense of humour not only to Will's father but to her daughters and her other sons. One family of Heath Robinson's cousins was exceptionally gifted, and might have become more famous than many of the professional humorists of their day had they been known by a wider audience than a small private circle of friends and relations; but they were neither artists nor writers, and so the memory of their Attic wit remains only with those who knew them personally.

Will's father, Thomas Robinson, began life as an apprentice to a watchmaker, but later on he took to wood engraving and finally he became an illustrator. Like other members of the family he felt the call of the sea, and in his boyhood he was so much bent on a nautical career that he seriously alarmed his mother. Hoping to discourage him from running away to sea she took him down to the docks where she found a sea captain who, she expected, would describe some of the grimmer, more realistic details of a sailor's lot; but to her dismay the perverse fellow painted a most rosy picture of life before the mast. The boy, of course, listened raptly. Perhaps the captain noticed her agonized expression for he broke off suddenly and asked young Thomas if he liked sugar.

" Yes," the boy replied eagerly.

The captain looked at him sadly and shook his head. " If there's one thing a sailor must *not* like, it's sugar," he said. " Now run along home and forget all about it."

After this Thomas Robinson seems to have given up the idea of the sea as a career and contented himself with making models of ships. But to show that the spirit of adventure was not entirely dead in him he indulged in a number of hair-raising exploits, one of which was to walk from end to end along the parapet of the old Highgate Archway.

At the time when Will first remembered him he had settled down to the somewhat exacting task of supporting a family of nine: his four sons, Tom, Charles, Will and George, his two daughters, Mary and Florence, with his wife, her sister and her young brother, George. Will said grandly that they had a general servant, a kitchen maid, a nurse, a housemaid and a cook, and then added: " As all these retainers were united in one person, our household was not greatly increased thereby." This compendious domestic support was a Peggotty type, and like Peggotty she came from Yarmouth.

Thomas Robinson's work lay with that popular weekly newspaper, the *Penny Illustrated*, which was started in 1861 and continued into the nineties when it was finally outmoded by the new journalism, more particularly the *Daily Graphic*.

The " P.I.P.," as it was affectionately called, was the first penny paper to bring illustrated news within the poor man's reach. Its Christmas numbers were immensely popular, and one of its scoops was to publish a picture of Jabez Spencer Balfour in March, 1893, which led to his arrest. Most of its illustrations were simply newspaper records of topical events reproduced by wood engravings. Some of them were taken from old numbers of the *Illustrated London News*, which for nearly forty years was edited by John Lash Latey. But this is not to say that it was lacking in enterprise. Its editor, John Latey Jnr., son of John Lash Latey, was a thoroughly live wire. He is of special interest to this biography because his daughter, Josephine, was to become Mrs. Heath Robinson.

Thomas Robinson was a pillar of the *Penny Illustrated*. For many years he contributed the front page illustration and an inside single page or double-spread. Gradually the readers came to recognize his work and looked for it every week. In those days the public wanted their weekly tot of melodrama over-proof, and Thomas was expected to serve out an intoxicating ration of battles, murders, fires, earthquakes, storms and wrecks at sea, as well as society functions and political sensations.

When it was a military event he relied on sketches sent in by Melton Prior, the war correspondent—a bald, highly strung man with a very high voice who was known as the " Screeching Billiard Ball "—but for other news he usually had to act as his own reporter. Often he spent more time and energy in collecting his material than on the final drawings.

At a moment's notice he would hurry off to the other end of the kingdom to make sketches of a railway accident, a mine disaster, a murder trial, or some other topical sensation. The Tay Bridge disaster was one of the jobs he was given; another was a fallen factory chimney in Bradford, and a third a fire in a theatre followed by a panic. His readers were not squeamish, and many a time poor Thomas had to portray details which revolted him. He drew sorrowing widows in mortuary scenes and tight-lipped coroners conducting unsavoury inquests. He visited scenes of sordid crimes, sketched suspected murderers with awful expressions of guilt and attended the funerals of the victims.

In London he had to be present at court trials, such as that of Piggott, the Irish journalist who wrote seditious letters which were published in *The Times,* purporting to have been written by Parnell; and of Mrs. Maybrick, who was convicted of murdering her husband, in a court crowded with Bank Holiday sightseers. His work was nearly always a race against the clock. Often he had to spend valuable time waiting in the courts to interview an important witness. Other times he went farther afield. It required great energy and physical strength to rush away on a Friday to the North of England or Scotland, return on Saturday and have an elaborate treatment of the subject ready for the engravers by Monday morning.

Sometimes important news would arrive for him on Saturday night, or even on Sunday morning, and the subject had to be illustrated, engraved, printed and published by Thursday. This was hard going. The surface on which the drawings were made was a set of boxwood blocks so closely screwed together that there was scarcely a trace of the joins. As soon as the drawing was done, the blocks were unscrewed and distributed to a staff of engravers. Their task completed, the blocks were joined together again and a master craftsman engraved over the joins.

This team work made for speed but it was rather trying for the unhappy illustrator. While Thomas worked at his drawing, an engraver might be standing impatiently by waiting to whisk the block away. If time was short he would seize the block and unscrew a large segment leaving the harassed artist with an irregularly shaped remnant to complete.

Will and his brothers took a keen family pride in their father's work. His reputation for accuracy was high. Had not a portrait of his, drawn from another's description, led to the arrest of Lefroy, who murdered Mr. Gold in a London–Brighton railway carriage? Most Saturday afternoons he would come home with his big black bag filled with drawing materials and wood blocks, and on Sunday morning he would be hard at work on his pictures for the week. With their hands clasped behind their backs, the little boys were allowed to look at those peculiar reporter's sketches, covered with written notes, which took the place of modern Press photographs.

It might be a blueprint of some murder drama, with the spot where the corpse was discovered carefully measured off and marked; or perhaps some stirring war dispatch from Melton Prior in Egypt; a bird's-eye view of the battlefield at Tel el Kebir, with the Egyptian army fleeing before Sir Garnet's gallant Highlanders; or the terrible slaughter of Baker Pasha's relief force at El Teb.

" We always watched keenly the development of my father's drawings," wrote Heath Robinson, " and our interest in the news of the day was thus kept continually alive. Sometimes we made drawings of the same events at his side. We knew all about the campaigns in Afghanistan and the Zulu wars. I could draw a passable Zulu, with feathered head-dress, long oval shield and assegai, at an early age. We were deeply stirred by the news of Isandhlwana and of Rorke's Drift, and were grieved at the death of the Prince Imperial. We had, I am afraid, a secret sympathy with that dethroned monarch, Cetewayo. Then there was the bad news of Majuba Hill. How we wished we could do something about it! We carefully followed in imagination the Khartoum relief expedition as it progressed stage by stage up the Nile. Finally the news that Khartoum was recaptured and Gordon avenged allowed us to breathe again."*

Thomas Robinson had his moments of triumph. The *Penny Illustrated* was a *John Bull* to the working man, and once on entering a railway signal box he was gratified to find its walls covered with his drawings.

Sometimes on Sunday mornings the boys were taken to see Uncle Charles, who lived not far away and who was doing similar work for the *Illustrated London News*. This journal was run on much the same lines as the *Penny Illustrated,* but it catered for a more educated class of reader. It had the enterprise to send out S. Reed, the first war correspondent, to the Crimea, which led to a rush of imitators. Uncle Charles was Thomas's only brother and his closest friend.

The Robinsons were always a most clannish family, and that different members of it could remain close friends until death, and even live together in perfect amity under the same roof, is evidence of that mildness and tolerance which was always so apparent in Will.

* *My Line of Life,* by W. Heath Robinson (Blackie).

CHAPTER II

THE HIGH ROAD OF ADVENTURE

OWING perhaps to plays such as *The Barretts of Wimpole Street* and to the well-known maternal strictness of Queen Victoria, many people imagine that children were treated with severity until the end of the nineteenth century. Some fathers, of course, were stern and some mothers were repressive, but by no means all of them. Even in the eighteenth century, when the gulf between parents and children was far wider, Locke wrote: " Most children's constitutions are either spoilt, or at least harmed, by cockering and tenderness."

By the eighteen eighties few parents were excessively strict. Children were expected to be seen and not heard, and when they asked too many questions they were told that curiosity killed the cat; they were cautioned against the sins of arguing with their elders and wasting time. But the pompous attitude of Age towards Youth was weakening, and natural affection was no longer stifled by stiff-necked condescension.

Young Will enjoyed his boyhood and was very fond of his parents. His life was much like that in most middle-class homes: regular, settled, unexciting, with familiar happenings endlessly repeated in a minor key. But evidently he did not think it uninteresting. All through his life he looked on the world with the eyes of a little boy who was ready to find adventure in the most trivial incident or, failing this, to manufacture one from his bright imagination.

It seems that Saturday was the day on which his hopes, and those of his brothers, Tom and Charles, were so glowingly set that to the end of his life the close of the week always brought with it a feeling of lively anticipation. Anything might happen on Saturday, for this was the day on which they were set free to seek adventure on the high road.

The other days of the week were mere stepping stones to the enchanted island. Monday was all that was humdrum and dull; perhaps this was the reaction from a Victorian Sunday. It was also wet as a rule, which shows how little things alter from one century to the next. But on Tuesday it obligingly cleared up for the washing. There was no waiting for the laundry van; everyone washed the household linen on Tuesday, and the wash-houses all down the road belched steam like the boilers of a battle fleet. Afterwards the gardens flaunted barrages of floating garments, which swelled up and threw themselves about with such unseemly abandon that they must have been shocking to Victorian eyes. Indeed, in families of strict propriety it was customary to dry intimate garments well out of sight.

By Thursday the coming Saturday's adventure was suffusing the sky with a golden glow, and on Friday night, which was bath night, the light of rising hope had begun to people the twilight with exciting phantoms. The boys saw themselves setting out along the Great North Road, that eternal highway of adventure along which Cumberland's troops had marched out to battle with the Young Pretender, and the Fencibles in their multi-coloured uniforms and inadequate weapons had come south to repel " Boney's " Grand Army. Dick Turpin and Dick Whittington had passed that way. Will always had a fellow feeling for Dick Whittington because like himself he must have been fond of cats. As everyone knows, human beings are divided into two very different categories: those who like cats and those who don't.

Setting out next morning, each boy with a parcel of sandwiches tied to his back, the goal would be High Barnet. Today, streams of trolleybuses knit up Barnet to the Metropolis, and the tattered buildings which wrap London like beggar's rags stretch to Potter's Bar. But at that time Barnet was a country village where a battle had once been fought, and it was possible, the boys thought, that a careful search might reveal weapons or pieces of armour. Moreover, the church at Hadley had a beacon all ready to be lit in the case of invasion. Perhaps they might catch a glimpse of the watchman, who of course must be standing there ready with his box of matches.

Walking briskly along the Holloway Road they would pass some of the old " knife-board " buses loaded up with the last batch of business passengers—grave City gentlemen in tall top-hats and long black coats. Passing the old Holloway Hall, in which bazaars and at times stormy political meetings were held—for politics were taken seriously in the eighties—the boys diverged from the main road along the Archway Road, which was a by-pass cutting through Highgate Hill to avoid the steep rise.

There was plenty to entertain them. If it were summer they might encounter a party of Irish who had come over to help with the harvest. A wild-looking lot, dressed in odd clothes, they all talked together at the tops of their voices in a brogue which you could hardly understand. Their small belongings they carried in blue and white check handkerchiefs dangling from their shoulders on the ends of sticks.

At this time there were hundreds of tramps on the roads. You often came upon a dirty, unshaven fellow, with a battered bowler perched on his matted hair, lighting a few sticks by the roadside to boil his billycan; or a poor, bedraggled slattern selling shoe laces or bags of dried lavender. Sometimes whole families were on the road with their bundles and teacans, begging as they went and sleeping in ditches or under the lea of haystacks. They called at your door and told you that their homes had been burnt down or made uninhabitable by floods, that they had been thrown out of work, or discharged unfit from hospital. You could never tell whether they spoke the truth, but to be on the safe side you gave them thick slices of bread plastered with lard, or a packet of cold potatoes, for which you received a whining " God bless ye, mum."

A little further on, the boys would see a smart barouche in which ladies with billowy silk dresses and dainty parasols fringed with chenille looked about them with raised eyebrows. Better still, a gentleman in tight knickerbockers and a pillbox cap would swerve down the road on his tall pennyfarthing bicycle. You might even meet a whole cycling club : troops of cyclists in close-fitting neat uniforms of dark blue or grey, with tight knee-breeches, like the young men in *Patience*. In front of them would ride a bugler to clear the way.

When you saw these newfangled machines approaching you kept well into the side of the road. The Sunday newspapers were always publishing stories of how somebody had been fatally injured by a bicycle. Letters from nervous readers called heaven to witness that the roads had been created for horse traffic and pedestrians, and they demanded that bicyclists should be banished to special roads of their own, like the railway trains. Other critics, struck by the agonized expressions of these performers, which was nicknamed " bicyclist's face," predicted that future generations of cyclists would be hunchbacked and fearfully distorted in their physiognomy.

Trudging on, Will and his brothers would reach the real country at Shepherd's Cot. It was from here, he wrote, that he saw Baldwin descend by parachute from a balloon over the grounds of the Alexandra Palace. And then he could not help adding: " It will be understood that I refer to the aeronaut and not to any other illustrious bearer of the name."

Beyond Highgate Woods, which filled the valley and rose to the hills on either side, they could see a marvellous panorama of open country dotted with the church towers of unspoilt villages. They stopped at the " Woodman " for a bottle of gingerade, though it was still early in the day, and ate sandwiches sitting on the grass. After this they struggled into Finchley. From here it was rather an anti-climax to turn back home without coming within miles of Barnet. But the Robinsons were indomitable optimists and they never doubted that one day they would reach their objective.

As a boy Heath Robinson was fascinated by butterflies, which were later to figure in his decorative work, and it is rather strange to think of him chasing them in Colney Hatch Lane. He was not the boy to harm even an insect, and when he described these adventures he was careful to explain that the butterflies sported with their hunters rather than the reverse. Once, towards the end of his life, he said to a friend: " Butterflies must be beautiful to each other as well as to us." Innately modest, he could not believe that the universe was created exclusively for Man.

Saturdays ended rather more sedately than they began, for in the evenings, when the days were long, each boy in turn would be taken by his parents for a walk to the Gate House on Highgate Hill—that favourite resort of the Cruikshank brothers. Perhaps " promenade " would be a better word, for although these excursions were looked forward to, they were rather stately occasions. The calm of a summer's evening was a very tempting time for a Victorian papa to moralize and improve his children's minds, and usually Thomas Robinson could not resist it. Will's responsibilities as a future citizen would be carefully impressed on him; his parents managed to give these walks an air of almost religious solemnity.

Luckily the human mind has several compartments, each of which can work independently of the rest. One of these in a small boy dutifully answers " yes " or " no " to the queries of a paternal exordium, leaving the other compartments free to take in the sharp impressions of childhood. The red-roofed St. Joseph's Retreat reminded him of a picture of a monastery in Switzerland. Beside it was Waterlow Park, and opposite the park was Oliver Cromwell's House with a grim studded door at the side. This invoked a whole flight of fancies. He could almost see the Protector riding out with a troop of Ironsides.

At the top of the hill stood the Gate House, with an ancient white gate which conjured up a picture of Dick Turpin astride Black Bess setting out on his famous ride to York. To the end of his life Will loved country walks, rustic inns, and the memory of the Gate House was always fresh in his mind. Passing along a dim passage, the Robinsons came to a hatch with a sliding window which was opened on their approach by a smiling old lady with black eyebrows and black ringlets. Behind her they could see shelves with black bottles of rum shrub and other liquors; each bottle bore a golden scroll with the name of the contents in black letters.

Directed by this lady to a little room with bow windows, they watched many other families outside taking their Saturday evening walk in the sedate manner of those days. A bald, stooping waiter, who no doubt served as a model for many a Heath Robinson drawing,

Courtesy of JOHN GLEDHILL, ESQ.

THE VICAR'S TEMPTATION

attended to their needs, and sometimes the landlady who was still in widow's weeds would come and talk about her husband who had died many years before.

Sunday was an altogether more formidable occasion. The starched clean collars were difficult to fasten and made dressing for the boys a tedious business; their best Sunday suits gave them a feeling of stiffness and restraint. Breakfasting late, they could see their neighbours walking primly to church or chapel, the fathers in top-hats, black frock-coats and striped trousers, the mothers with parasols, and the children following rather disconsolately, each member of the party carrying a hymn book or prayer book. The young Robinsons could look out on this scene with composure since their father was busy with his illustrations and their mother, who was no bigot, only insisted that they should attend one service in the evening.

Like most good mothers, she was chiefly concerned with the Sunday dinner. The ticking of the jack and the delicious smell of cooking was one of those keen memories of youth which never faded. Stout and ale came from a pub nearby. A potman brought it to the door in foaming cans which were afterwards hung on the area railings to be called for. The Robinsons were a little too exalted in the social scale to go and fetch it themselves.

Will always remembered a guest who sometimes came to these Sunday luncheons. He was long-nosed, shy and silent, with great flowing moustaches joined to short side whiskers. He wore a light check suit, and a brilliant pin glittered in his tie. Such were the beaux of those days.

When evening came the boys were allowed to choose their own place of worship. Who could forget the weariness and tedium of church services in the eighties: the cold, damp, earthy odour of the unheated church, the frowning pews of the bigwigs, the nicely graded congregation, the parson's droning voice, a woman occa-

H.R.—B

sionally fussing with her hair, or a man easing his tight collar, the sermon which went on and on into the infinite drowsy distance?

Will was too observant, too impressionable to be bored even in a church. He preferred the top gallery of a three-decker church from where he could look down at the floors below. What would happen, he wondered, if somone were to drop a hassock on to the head of the droning clergyman? It was a red-letter day when a hymn book actually did drop from the gallery on to the worshippers! Sometimes the boys fidgeted so much that the shawled and bonneted crones who acted as pew openers turned them out, and they had to wander away and find some other church; but usually they sat or knelt immersed in their own reflections until the service came to a merciful end.

In the eighties children were obliged to listen for as much as an hour to sermons which depended on the temperament of the preacher. Eternal punishment was still a favourite theme, and so was an uncomfortably materialistic Heaven which seemed like an apotheosis of the Machine Age. In spite of the rising tide of Radicalism, another subject was the supreme rightness of the existing social order. Most of the congregation slumbered or daydreamed, and the moment the sermon was over, sprang to their feet like jacks-in-a-box to sing the final hymn with a gusto most unflattering to the preacher.

Will enjoyed the singing, and at one time he and Tom were choirboys in a little corrugated iron church in the Hornsey Road. Tom and Charles had ordinary voices, but Will had quite a pleasant one which gave his friends pleasure when he was grown up. Characteristically he sang with a vehemence which was more suited to a sea shanty or a drinking chorus than to the sentimental ditties which he sometimes attempted.

As to sermons and prayers, established religion never made much impression on him until towards the end of his life. Something happened then which came as a considerable shock to him, something which made him modify his ideas.

CHAPTER III

THE LOOM OF YOUTH

IT is strange that we fear machines as the destroyers of paid employment but have little fear of them as the destroyers of creative endeavour. Hardly anyone has attacked industrialism because it makes us too comfortable, removes necessary obstacles. Living adventurously is at a discount. We have all grown rather tired.

Two wars and innumerable crises have been too much for us. We expect ready-made entertainment without the effort of having to contrive it for ourselves; books, newspapers and magazines which need little concentration; armchair vehicles to convey us in effortless ease; predigested philosophy; art explained in illustrated monthly instalments; fireside religion with the sting drawn, offering us guaranteed salvation. In preparation for this we do our best to remove the very difficulties on which our children should be cutting their teeth.

Heath Robinson always said that he and his brothers owed much to their early days at home where they had to provide their own entertainment and manufacture many of their own toys. Thereby their imaginations were continually exercised and they were obliged to become craftsmen. Having no clockwork steamships or electric trains, they did their best to create something of the sort from wood and tin, string and pieces of wire. Clumsy as their efforts were, often leading to ludicrous results, they sowed the seeds of something important.

Tom, Charles and Will all drew nearly as soon as they could walk, and their father consistently encouraged them. Often they would draw on their slates, telling some imaginary dramatic story in a series of pictures. Of course they would be influenced by the work they had seen their father do. Battles, fires, shipwrecks appeared on their slates; or perhaps, some boyish conception of a hero's adventures with a strong supporting cast of robbers, pirates and castaways.

Still more important to Will's career was the construction of toy theatres. Toy theatres seem to be specially attractive to humorous artists in their boyhood. At a school in Leeds Phil May once contrived marvellous scenery and the most elaborate characters for a toy theatre built by himself and several of his schoolfellows. A sheet of tin produced peals of thunder and a large humming-top simulated the distant tones of a cathedral organ. He and his friends even staged *Pepper's Ghost,* using an ingenious arrangement of glass screens and mirrors.

Helped by their Uncle George, the Robinson brothers were every bit as enterprising. They wrote their own plays and designed the scenery. Their Christmas pantomimes took weeks of preparation. There were trap-doors for the sudden entrances and exits of demons and fairies, drop-curtains, dozens of tiny candles for the lighting, and many other stage props. A theatre of their own making gave considerable scope for their ingenuity, and most probably this was one of the things which later on gave Will such a quick grasp of constructional details. He said that home life did more for him than all the hours he spent at school.

All three brothers had a strong dramatic imagination. Tom relates how they would be sitting round the table of a winter's evening, absorbed in their homework or their drawing, or perhaps preparing a pantomime for the big new stage which Uncle George had helped them build. Suddenly the silence of the dark street outside would be broken by a sort of growling in the distance with something of a threat in its tone, gradually swelling to the raucous bellow of a newspaper boy shouting about a horrible murder in Holloway.

Filled with fascinated curiosity, they send their servant out to buy a paper. They are lucky if a paper of the previous day is not palmed off on them; and even if it is the current issue, there is rarely any mention of a crime! However, they refuse to admit that they have been " had." Somewhere in the neighbourhood they feel sure that a corpse is lying in a pool of blood, and not far away a murderer is hiding in some dark doorway.

Owing, it may be, to some lingering love of the sea, Thomas Robinson had pitched on a dwelling between the houses of two sea captains. Each of these captains had sons who exerted a strong influence on the Robinson boys, intensifying the romantic atmosphere with which they surrounded themselves. Their conversation was always of the sea and of ships. They spoke of their fathers' exciting voyages, embroidering a little, perhaps; they also allowed the Robinson boys to help them rig model ships and handle nautical gear-blocks and ropes and ships' lanterns.

On several thrilling occasions one of the two fathers, Captain White, took the boys with his own sons down to the docks where they spent the day aboard his ship. Those were days which they never forgot. They wandered blissfully about the lovely clipper as she shipped her cargo for a year's voyage, perhaps to New Zealand. They yarned with the mates and the steward, and they dined with the captain in his cabin. One such day was worth a year of commonplace existence. After it even their games with ships became something more than mere pretence.

Their father bought a cartload of odd timbers—poles, laths and beams of many different sizes. Heaped in the garden, they were an obvious temptation to the boys. They built ships, railway engines and explorers' huts.

A big packing case covered with boards for a deck, two poles for mast and bowsprit, a tablecloth for a sail, and they were well afloat. Strictly conscientious sailors, when their mother called them in to dinner, they never failed to furl the sail and lay the ship to anchor—usually in what they called the " offing." It was a point of honour not to leave the ship by merely stepping out on to the gravel path. The thing was done by using two boards and a pole. One board represented the side of the ship and the other the quay, and by a series of complicated movements they disembarked dry-foot and with their illusion unbroken.

They were just as particular with their railway engine, running it in conformity with a timetable and stopping at every station on the route to Brighton or Ramsgate. One of the brothers, being enamoured of a girl at his school (though she was all unconscious of the honour) decided to build a real boat and entice her away to some Isles of the Blessed on the distant seas. The other two were quite ready to collaborate; their pocket money was spent on nails, and for days on end they hammered away until some spoil-sport pointed out that the nearest navigable water was six or seven miles off and that water had a habit of seeping through half-inch gaps in planks. This shattered the illusion. Their romantic project was abandoned, and the boat became the roof of an explorer's hut in the Arctic Circle.

At a certain age most boys fix their admiration on some older friend and invest him with compendious powers of insight and penetration. If anything puzzling occurred to the Robinsons, the obvious oracle to consult was the son of a sea captain. Now Will shared a bed with Tom in a bedroom at the top of their three-storeyed house, and one night, to their dismay, the door mysteriously opened. The boys clutched each other in terror. In the pitch dark they could see nothing, but they heard shuffling footsteps which approached their bed. " Who's that? " Tom gasped; a queer sound rather like a growl was the only answer. The ghostly footsteps pattered round the bed and out of the room. They heard the door close and at length fell asleep.

Next morning the peculiar imagination of the Robinson family pictured the ghostly visitor as a tall, dark man whose ugly face was concealed by a black visor, and Tom suddenly remembered having seen a lantern standing outside the door with a fierce dog beside it. What more natural than to confide this horrid occurrence to the son of a sea captain? They hoped that he would not dismiss it with some mundane explanation, and sure enough he did not. But he could not allow his father's adventures to be overshadowed. During a terrible storm, he told the awe-struck boys, the captain's ship had been nearly wrecked; but even the fear of imminent death was obliterated by the sight of fireballs falling from the heavens. What is more, each of these balls contained the image of an angel! Since, as his father told him, it is seldom given to sinful man to behold good angels, the fireball spirits were probably evil, and on the same reasoning the ghostly midnight visitor with the black visor was also evil.

Both Tom and Will felt the need for the Mysterious, and if supernatural happenings were in short supply they contrived them just as they contrived the effects for their toy theatre. A picture on the wall, an illustration in a book, or a dark corner of the staircase was enough to touch off their imaginations. Even if an event were capable of the simplest explanation it would often set their young fancies to work so tellingly that they would come to believe their own fairy tales.

Sometimes when there were more plausible reasons for delusion the boys succeeded in frightening themselves quite seriously. Once this happened after the sudden death of Mr. Bingle, the sweep. He would come early in the morning before the boys were up, and from their bedroom they could hear the rattle of his brooms and canes in the chimney. One morning these sounds ceased abruptly, and soon afterwards they heard a great commotion.

Panic drew them downstairs in their nightshirts, and in the passage they saw their servant, Esther, tearfully explaining matters to a policeman. She had found Mr. Bingle " lyin' all of a heap on the floor in a dead faint." Presently the family doctor came out of the kitchen and announced that the unfortunate sweep. had burst a blood vessel while at his work and passed away.

Mrs. Bingle was sent for and presently arrived in a large befeathered hat and a coloured shawl, with pendants hanging from her ears. She was not at all perturbed and deftly searched the dead man's pockets, explaining that he had sold a horse the previous night. There was an inquest and a most imposing funeral generously attended by costers, horse copers, small tradesmen and the upper stratum of the local gipsies. The funeral party rode in a curious assortment of pony carts, growlers and converted tradesmen's vans. At the tail end of the cortège was a pearly king in a hansom cab driven by a cabby whose top-hat was wreathed in black crêpe. In honour of the Robinson family the procession passed by their house.

All this produced such an impression on the boys that when, a few nights later, Tom and Will heard the ghostly rattle of the sweep's broom in the chimney they were in agony of alarm and pulled the bedclothes over their heads. Esther, when consulted next morning, confirmed their worst fears and volunteered the terrifying information that " all sweeps' ghosts is black."

Several peaceful nights had begun to reassure them a little, when one evening they again heard the ghostly rattle in the chimney. However, next morning the ghost of Mr. Bingle was exorcized by the discovery of a dead bird lying beneath the kitchen chimney in a little heap of dust!

Both brothers fed their imagination on the books of their day—books by Captain Marryat, Harrison Ainsworth, Talbot Baines Reed, Anstey, and Rider Haggard. Boys' books in those days were sold in coloured paper covers for fourpence halfpenny.

Sometimes they would be given money to buy a birthday book, and they would rummage in Holywell Street, popularly known as Booksellers' Row. This was one of London's oldest streets, a narrow passage-way overhung by gabled houses and monopolized by the booksellers. Ragged, barefoot urchins sold newspapers or turned cartwheels, begging for pennies. Italian organ grinders played while girls in tight black bodices and big feathered hats sedately danced. It was almost mediæval in its antiquity. Nobody was in a hurry; its patrons were mostly elderly men of leisure who seemed to relish the lack of ventilation and the smell of old books. They browsed like horses coming to drink over the troughlike wooden boxes into which the books had been thrown. To the boys many of these books seemed dull enough, but among the sermons and the statistics, the moral discourses and the economic treatises, you might have the luck to find something exciting. And although at the time they did not know it, you could pick up startling bargains in the antique shops which were overflowing with goods. Among heaps of miscellaneous junk you might buy for a few shillings priceless drawings by Blake, Gainsborough or Rowlandson.

Tom was always the accepted authority on literature, and his younger brother usually accepted his advice without question. *The Castle of Ehrenstein,* which was one of his choices, inspired Tom to confide in Will that he had made a marvellous discovery: their house was built on top of an ancient haunted castle! He even blindfolded Will and took him on a tour to the banqueting hall, the dungeons and the torture chambers.

A feeling for the Unknown, a taste for the Mysterious, was as necessary for the future caricaturist of the Machine Age as the ability to see something ludicrous in mechanical processes; for the new habit of thought which came with industrialization was doing its best to banish the Ineffable and explain everything in heaven and earth in terms of the commonplace. Earlier generations knew well enough that they lived in a world of effects and that unseen forces were at work behind the scenes. They called these forces gods, demons, norns, devas, trulls, fairies, undines, brownies, and many other names, and as in the case of Tom and Will it was not long before their imagination " materialized " these abstract ideas into visible shapes.

Modern scientific thought, machine worship, has almost killed these beliefs. If it had stopped short at abolishing witch hunting, the belief that brownies, not bacilli, infect tainted milk, and other such ignorant superstitions, this would have been all to the good; but unhappily belief in the Unknown was cast off along with belief in crude fantasies. In positivist thought, all the intangibles are ironed out, and everything is held to be explicable in terms of matter and motion; all is matter-of-fact, logical, utilitarian. The shadowy inhabitants of Olympus and Magonia were swept away with a wave of the Victorian lecturer's hand, and their places were filled by mechanical monsters of which nobody could possibly fail to be aware.

At the same time Science turned its back on imaginative insight. " In the Middle Ages," wrote Emile Mâle, " the idea of a thing which a man formed for himself was always more real than the actual thing itself, and we see now why these mystical centuries had no conception of what men call science. The study of things for their own sake held no meaning for the thoughtful man. . . . The task for the student of nature was to discern the eternal truth that God would have each thing express."*

This is putting the matter in religious terms, but it shows how differently our ancestors looked at the world, and how low individual insight has sunk in the scale of values in comparison with so-called scientific " facts." Modern scientific thought hardly has its eye on eternal truth at all; it deals in narrow specialized aspects, small branches of fact broken off the Tree of Life. Grappling with ponderous masses of data it produces results which although triumphs of logical skill are nevertheless mice compared with the mountains of mental machinery involved.

All this was one day to be caricatured by Heath Robinson.

* *Religious Art in France, XIII Century*—by Emile Mâle.

CHAPTER IV

SCHOOLDAYS IN THE EIGHTIES

IN the seventies and eighties teaching young children was still a favourite means of eking out a livelihood for poor clergymen and needy spinsters. Few of the Dames schools of those days treated children imaginatively, and the teaching was sometimes very poor indeed. Young Heath Robinson's first school was in the hands of a Miss Mole and her mother, a bent old lady in a white cap and a dark apron who read her pupils *Mavor's Spelling Book* and other pleasant stories, and allowed them plenty of time to amuse themselves with drawing on their slates. The maternal instinct of these two ladies found relief in fussing over Miss Mole's brother, a foppish young man who wore a top-hat, a frock-coat and light kid gloves when he went off to the City in the mornings. The children regarded him with awe.

Tom and Charles were already at a more advanced school, and when he was a little older Will joined them there. This school was about a mile from their home and to reach it they had to pass a row of white posts. Beyond these posts the neighbourhood sank lower and lower in the social scale until it grounded in a sort of Alsatia. Its inhabitants were a rough, uncouth crowd of Irish Wastrels and beggars living in the most squalid poverty. Probably they were a remnant of that gin-soaked underworld described by Dickens which was only then passing away.

In *Our Mutual Friend*, Dickens says: " His house was in the Holloway region, north of London, and then divided from it by fields and trees. Between Battle Bridge and that part of the Holloway district in which he dwelt, was a tract of suburban Sahara where tiles and bricks were burnt, bones were boiled, carpets were beaten and rubbish was shot, dogs were fought, and dust was heaped by contractors."

The boys made the journey twice a day, except on rainy days when they took their lunch to school, and they hurried nervously past the slum. Luckily for them the inhabitants were rarely aggressive except among themselves, so they were not molested. But on their way to school they would frequently pass through a crowd of bloated husbands and wives at the height of a family feud. This was conducted so publicly that it was an open event in which anyone could join. Sometimes they had to push their way through a circle of hoarse, swearing men and screaming women swaying round the two principal combatants who were smashing each other's faces to pulp with their bare fists. The boys would hurry on, a little scared, thinking how very red was the blood on the dead white faces against the dingy background of the crowd.

There was a great deal of fighting with bare fists in those days. At the end of the Robinsons' garden was a high brick wall, between which and the untidy yards of the shops in Holloway Road lay a few acres of meagre grass. This was known as " Carpet Grounds," and here on Saturday afternoons and Sunday mornings many a bloody combat was fought to a finish. The boys had a good view of these fights from their upper windows, and they saw desperate battles between pitch-and-toss gamblers who often came to blows.

At their school, too, the boys settled their quarrels by combat. A challenge would be thrown out and accepted; a meeting place would be arranged, usually a long way from the school. At the appointed hour the fight would be conducted in strict accordance with such rules as the boys knew. Seconds timed the rounds, and everything was carried out as in an exhibition bout, except for the roped-off ring. As far as Tom's memory goes, Will never had a fight; no one saw him bear the customary scars. His was always a gentle disposition, very different from that of most boys of his day.

The school building consisted of three dwelling houses joined together, and there being no playground the boys were obliged to play in the streets. Their games were adapted to the conditions: there were games with marbles and peg-tops, and a kind of double tip-cat game called " Wogle," which was played in much the same way as cricket. Some of their games, such as " Jolly Little Knacker," belonged to the old chanting games which are now mostly forgotten.

There was also an exciting game known as " Buttons," which was played by pitching brace buttons from the kerb on to the lines forming the joints of the paving stones. If you lost your stock of buttons you cut some more from your trousers; and if you lost *them,* you had to go home with your hands in your pockets to keep your trousers up!

Some members of the school staff were evidently pro-totypes of those solemn, baldheaded gentlemen who figured later in the Heath Robinson humorous draw-ings. In most schools there are masters who ride some hobby-horse, and are much encouraged by the boys, who prefer a talk, however dull, to the necessity of working. One such enthusiast at the Robinsons' school was an elderly party who could prove beyond all pos-sible manner or shadow of doubt that Man was des-cended not from the ape but from the bear. In spite of a shortsightedness which often caused him to punish the wrong boy, he was so popular that when he announced his impending retirement at the end of the term, the boys presented him with a gold watch. However, when they reasembled after the holidays he was there just the same and continued to propound his evolutionary theories.

Always charitable, Heath Robinson tried to review the school's services to him in the kindliest possible light; but the most he could give it credit for having taught him was reading, writing, elementary arithmetic and a little history, geography and science. Only one teacher inspired him with any desire to learn. This was the schoolmistress who taught him electricity and magnetism. Half humorously, he said that if he had stayed on at the school he might have become a great scientist. Before he died, a great many people who had never met him thought that he *was* one—a scientist with a kink.

Education has only recently become methodical, and in those days it was struggling out of the morass of earlier times when even butchers, barbers and bankrupts turned schoolmaster, and illiterate ushers were frequently the laughing stock of the school. A master, certainly a headmaster, was expected to have some learning even in a mixed school; but little attempt was made to capitalize the eager curiosity of youth or to invest the efforts of the most sensitive and impressionable years in long-term securities.

It is unfair to blame the school for not seeing in young Will a future artist of international fame; but even if it had done so the staff was totally inadequate to deal with such a boy. The art teacher was the head, a portly gentleman with many letters after his name, whose dignified bearing and majestic presence filled most of the boys with awe; but if the great man was otherwise engaged, then the art master was any other teacher who happened to be free. Perhaps this did not matter very much since all the boys had to do was to copy landscapes and rural details from special books published for this purpose. Some of them were not bad; they were compiled from studies by the Old Masters. Will enjoyed the work and there are traces of this early training in some of his rural sketches.

If the school was not very strong in education it was at least conducted with great dignity. On the summons "All in!" at half-past nine, the boys climbed the stairs into the school and hung up their caps and coats in what was once the greenhouse. Having taken their seats in the various classrooms, the little girls would troop in sedately, for it was a mixed school. During the morning lessons the headmaster's wife would make a stately progress through the school to collect any fees that were due. If your fees were much overdue she might order you to go home and fetch them!

The headmaster always maintained his dignity. Even when he invited boys to tea he would read some learned work amid the clatter of tea cups. He called his school a college and would march his boys in military formation through the streets to the hall where the annual concerts and prizegivings were held. There were no such things as school ties in those days, but he insisted on his pupils wearing mortarboards. Other schools in the neighbourhood evidently considered this a sign of snobbery and would sometimes wage guerilla warfare, though hostilities seldom came to more than long-distance bombardments with stones.

In 1884 Will joined Tom and Charles at a more expensive school where most of the masters had university degrees and wore caps and gowns when teaching. This was the Islington High School which was known then as the Probationary School of Islington. Its object, according to the grandiloquent rules, was " to provide a Course of Education for Youth, to comprise Classical Learning, the Modern Languages, Mathematics, and such other branches of Useful Knowledge as may be advantageously introduced; together with religious and moral instruction, in conformity with the doctrines and discipline of the Church of England."

This sounded well enough, but it was Heath Robinson's misfortune all through his schooldays to miss the beginning and foundation of his subjects and for ever to be starting in the middle of them so that he could never catch up with the rest of his class. Though willing to learn and ready to be interested, the right stimulus never came. Any rudiments of the classics and the sciences which he picked up he largely forgot by the time he was grown up, and he said afterwards that much of the time he spent at school was thrown away.

The new school and the family's removal to a bigger house in the Camden Road at about this time must have coincided with some increment in Thomas Robinson's salary. The boys at Islington High School were of a different class: sons of doctors, professional men and others with jobs in the City, and a large sprinkling of wealthy Jews who lived by their synagogue in Canonbury. On the other hand, the boys at their earlier school were mostly sons of local tradesmen. So evident was this that you could tell the calling of a boy's father by the sense of smell alone. Besides a well-greased head, which seemed common among butchers' families, a penetrating odour of suet hung about one boy to confirm suspicions. Another boy, the son of a provision merchant, exuded scents of cheese and butter. The most pungent of all was the son of an oilmonger whose morning wash might have been taken in paraffin!

However, all three brothers probably got a good deal more out of this humble school than from the more select one in Islington. They were not the type for an establishment which aped public school standards without really achieving them; they were more at home in a school which, however humble, allowed them some freedom of expression. Islington High School directed any individual characteristics into prepared channels and then stifled them by traditional methods of treatment. Will was not understood, nor was much attempt made to understand him. If the learned school staff could have looked into the future and seen some of the work which made him famous, they would probably have been nonplussed, perhaps even horrified.

In spite of some improvement in their finances the Robinsons were not very well off; there was not enough money to pay for the midday meal provided by the school, nor even to allow the boys more than a few pence to buy a scone and a cup of coffee. Will envied the boys who could have their meals at the school. The sandwiches which he took with him were rather unsatisfying when a tantalizing odour of cooking stole across the playground at midday. Looking back on those days it seemed to him that much of his discontent and lack of effort was due to underfeeding.

But after a time help came through his friendship with a boy named Fred Bernard Smith, whose mother owned a business near the school from which every day she provided a good solid meal to the school staff. Her son had his dinner there, and one day Will was invited to join him. Probably she was quick to notice how eagerly he tucked in to the roast mutton and roly-poly pudding stuffed with strawberry jam, because the invitation soon became an open one. Mrs. Smith's kindness was never forgotten, and Fred remained a life-long friend.

Another friend of those days was Richard Walthew, the composer, whose more popular works include his duet setting of " It was a Lover and his Lass," and his music for the comic opera *The Enchanted Island,* which has been broadcast several times. Walthew was more particularly a friend of Tom's and would often visit the Robinson home where he would play some of his compositions on the piano. One of his earliest efforts was a musical setting of " The Pied Piper," but Will particularly enjoyed singing his " Eldorado." For twenty-five years he was music professor at Queen's College, Harley Street, which was the first ladies' college.

The advent of Walthew into the family circle made a considerable difference in the cultural outlook of the boys, especially in music. Before they knew him their enthusiasm for music was faint and their taste rather crude. Their father talked a good deal of *Maritana, La Bohème, Traviata,* and other operas of his young days without arousing much interest in his sons. He insisted on all his family being taught music, but in time they wearied of the eternal scales and exercises and the uninspiring tunes from their music books which they were allowed to strum. But with the arrival of Walthew, all this was changed. He introduced them to Beethoven, Mozart, Wagner and Chopin, and opened their minds to what music could mean for them. In later years something of Walthew's influence went into Will's delicate handling of his illustrations to Shakespeare, *The Water Babies,* Hans Andersen and other books in the more imaginative vein.

Sharing Walthew's enthusiasm meant going to the opera, either with him or with Fred Smith, who had become very much interested in music. There were no theatre queues in those days and a good deal depended on luck, and perhaps muscular strength. When the doors opened the close-packed crowd became an unruly mob. You pushed your way up the stairs, sometimes in the most unseemly manner, and once past the ticket office you raced up flights of stone stairs—right to the top, if you were in " the gods." Having got a seat, you looked round, probably with mixed feelings. You regretted that you had not won a seat in the front row, and often you were depressed that your view of the stage was blotted out by the enormous cartwheel hat of the lady sitting in front of you.

Will was very fond of Highbury Place, where his friend lived. Many interesting people have lived there. One of them, Abraham Newland, chief cashier of the Bank of England, whose signature was for many years attached to the bank notes, lived at number 38, the home of Richard Walthew. He died in 1838. " Prior to September in that year he had slept for twenty-five years at his apartments in the Bank without absenting himself for a single night. After the business at the Bank in his department had ended, he had taken his modest repast, his carriage was brought, and was constantly ordered to Highbury, in the vicinity of Islington, where he drank tea at a small cottage. Those who live in that neighbourhood will recollect his daily walk, hail, rain or sunshine, along the row of buildings called Highbury Place, and on his return to his carriage his uniform tribute of gratitude to his large unwieldy horses, he always crossing the way and patting them, however uncleanly the road, and however inclement the weather."*

At that time Highbury Place was the exclusive dwelling place of rich City merchants and other people of wealth and consequence, and its beautiful Georgian houses were some of the finest on the outskirts of London. Even in the eighties it was an oasis of calm after the rattle and roar of Upper Street and Holloway Road. Many of the inhabitants were still moneyed men of leisure, and from their windows they looked out on to a peaceful meadow with grazing sheep.

Sometimes Will would visit another friend in Highbury Place: Percy Billinghurst, who lived a few doors

* *The Life of Abraham Newland.*

away from the Walthews. He would go to his home and listen to his old blind father playing the organ, walk in the garden and look at the mulberry tree of which his friend was very proud, and drink ale drawn from a cask in the deep cellars down below. Later, when he began his career he shared a studio with Billinghurst, also the high hopes and bitter disappointments which is the fate of most young artists.

CHAPTER V

FESTIVALS AND FUNERALS

THE Robinson family at this time moved in a mixed society which included people of many professions. There were sea captains and innkeepers, goldsmiths and bookbinders, and some pleasant fellows who followed no profession at all, or at any rate none for very long. Thomas Robinson's work brought him in contact with journalists, artists, one of them was Birket Foster, and wood engravers. His employer and particular friend, John Latey, Jnr., knew many of the artists and literary men of his day. Earlier he had known Charles Dickens and his family and many other writers of the past.

The Robinsons were great Dickensians, and they often chafed at the charge which was brought against Dickens for exaggerating his characters. Far from exaggerating, it seemed to them that he had drawn direct from life, for the people of their own acquaintance had even more clearly marked characteristics.

There was Tom K., for instance, who made and repaired umbrellas in his little shop in the Pentonville Road. He and his family lived over their shop in rooms so small that it was a mystery where they put themselves. Yet it was a joy to visit them, for they were always laughing over some joke which they were anxious to share with their visitors.

There were many others, each with some distinct Dickensian oddity; jewellers and watchmakers living over their shops and workrooms in Clerkenwell with a contentment which would have been inexplicable but for some freakish twist of optimism. One gentleman of their acquaintance looked like a bag of bones and parchment and habitually wore so melancholy an expression that instinct prompted you to run away when you saw him coming. Yet he always accosted Thomas Robinson with the news that every day he encountered something which made life more beautiful and increased his trust in his fellow men! He would then hobble off with great cheerfulness as if in search of further blessings.

Then there was Mr. Parker, the knobbly headed cobbler and bootmaker, who would call at the house with his wares on Saturday evening, drink a bottle of stout with the family while they were at supper, and entertain them with his quaint views and philosophy. He was very much interested in Will, in whom he seemed to discern something which distinguished him from the others. Another quaint old man, a gospeller, presented Mr. Robinson with a copy of his book, *Man*, every other sentence of which was drawn from the Scriptures. When not at his Concordance he made rustic summerhouses and garden seats.

Among the artist friends of the family was J. Mahoney, a peppery Irishman, who, despite frequent and violent quarrels with Thomas, always remained faithful. Joseph Pennell considered that his drawings in the *Sunday Magazine* were equal to anything that had ever been done in England. For the " Household Edition " of Dickens issued in the early seventies, Mahoney drew twenty-eight pictures for *Oliver Twist* and fifty-eight for *Little Dorrit* and *Our Mutual Friend*. He also did the drawings for Whymper's *Scrambles in the Alps*, a book much prized by collectors.

Love of the variety in human beings is something which Heath Robinson inherited in a marked degree.

One of his strongest traits was his sympathy with what he called " ordinary people." He saw the good in everyone and he had no patience with theories and doctrines which underlined the rottenness of human nature. This feeling coloured his character and it is evident in much of his work.

In these days of mass entertainment and swift transport the mind is numbed with a surfeit of impressions, few of which sink into the memory, but sixty years ago even the most trivial happenings meant a great deal because they were more fully digested. In adult life Heath Robinson looked back on his boyhood and remembered many small incidents which had helped to sharpen his imagination and shape his peculiar sense of humour.

He chuckled at the memory of his Uncle George gloriously attired in his dark green uniform and spiked helmet for the annual Easter Review of the Volunteers, or the Field Day on Brighton Downs. At the time this was far from a laughing matter; the boys were tremendously impressed watching the women of the household tighten his belts and straps, adjust his great pack, and fill up his waterbottle with cold tea. Will, with his horror of cruelty, shuddered to think of the triple-edge bayonet lunging at human flesh, and he was quite convinced that the spiked helmet was specially designed for butting at the enemy.

He also remembered the Victorian funeral parties which combined seedy pomp with thinly disguised relish of the gloomy proceedings. Funerals in the eighties were an opportunity for family reunions in state, and their touch of sombre drama was part of the chiaroscuro of family life. Who could forget the funeral guests, speaking in hushed voices, sitting stiffly in the little parlour which smelt strongly of cigars and the best black rapee? A ghostly light filtered through the lowered venetian blinds and the drawn lace curtains; the backs of the armchairs were protected from the oily heads of the male guests by crochet-work antimacassars; all was gloom, save for some bottles of stimulating liquor on the sideboard.

Many of the family's relations, half forgotten or complete strangers, bore biblical names as if expressly for the occasion. To the children they must have been an almost fabulous congregation. All were in stygian black. The gentlemen wore long black frock-coats and wide trousers, and their heads were supported by the deepest hard collars which chafed their necks. Looped across each waistcoat was a heavy gold watchchain and seal, and beside each chair was a chimney-pot hat circled with a broad band of crêpe. The ladies had deeply flounced dresses with high bustles, and perched on their tall coiffures were little toques or bonnets; but you were chiefly aware of a coarse black crêpe which seemed as rough as emery paper.

Some of the guests so exactly fitted the occasion that young Will thought they must spend their lives attending funerals. He always remembered a distant cousin, a bookbinder by profession, whom he imagined as born in mourning, nursed in long black clothes and bonnet, and when grown up doing a little undertaking as a hobby. It was impossible to think of him as anything but funereal, for even his eyebrows, moustache and short whiskers were in mourning.

The whole family, children included, went to the funeral ceremony. The gentlemen assumed expressions even more solemn, the ladies lowered their long black veils, and they all took their places in the carriages. The hearse, drawn by fat black horses with ostrich plumes, was a block box on wheels, with black knobs at each corner. Awed but thrilled, the boys drove with the family at walking pace, preceded by the undertaker who stalked down the road like a solemn crow. Will marvelled at how the crowds they passed could go about their daily business unconcerned.

As they drew near the cemetery, the cemetery bell beckoned them on with its mournful monotone, and inside the cemetery gates stone angels wept at the urns. Passing the vaults and the mausoleums, which seemed like the entrances to some celestial suburbia, Will imagined knockers and letter-boxes on their front doors and wondered who kept the latchkeys. The dreary church cast a pall on his spirits and dimmed the prospect of a bright hereafter in a chilly twilight of pessimism. The overworked clergyman who rattled perfunctorily through the burial service and disappeared without a word of sympathy emphasized the hollowness of the ceremony; and the miraculous disappearance of grief among the funeral party, which was more pronounced after a visit to the " Bald-faced Stag " on the way home, must have made an observant child see that the real feelings of grown-up people do not always tally with their behaviour.

If Heath Robinson had chosen to become a satirist, his technical skill might have made him a great one. But a satirist must have something bitter in his temperament, and this he lacked. Looking back on those funerals, he must have seen the humour in the contrast between outward solemnity and inward satisfaction; at all counts, this contrast became one of the corner stones on which his humorous work was built.

He was never much interested in politics or controversial matters. On the other hand he possessed a " fey " streak which remained with him all his life. He was always the little boy wandering inquisitively through the world, intensely interested in what he saw but not much inclined to criticize except with the gentlest humour.

One day in his early youth he went to Epping Forest on his annual Sunday School treat. Eight or nine wagonettes decked with flags and streamers and brightly striped awnings, overflowing with children who sat on long benches facing one another, set off gaily, followed by a crowd of ragged boys who ran along behind them. Arriving at their destination, Will found that an elaborate programme of sports and games had been arranged for the afternoon. But for him the forest was more attractive than the chance of winning a prize, and while the teachers were busily superintending the games he slipped away by himself.

For hours he wandered blissfully among the great trees, but when he tried to retrace his steps he found that he was lost. He was overcome with fright, which increased when he saw a pair of round eyes staring at him from behind a bush. However, it turned out to be nothing more alarming than a country boy who led him to his cottage; and the boy's mother gave him a glass of milk and guided him back to his companions.

Such boys as Will nearly always avoid the commonplace amusements of their fellows and, discovering some private fairyland, create a little world of their own. When he stayed at Brighton, which was very different from the noisy, crowded Brighton of today, his favourite playground was the old Chain Pier. A pier, of course, to a nautically minded boy is a battleship. This one had many masts and flagstaffs to help the illusion, and in rough weather it even swayed slightly as if it were afloat. True, it is unusual to buy brandy balls and bulls-eyes aboard one of His Majesty's men of war, and it is seldom that the crew offer you pin cushions and workboxes decorated with coloured shells; but imagination can turn the blind eye as easily as it can open the sighted one, and to Will even the bandstand looked like the work of a shipwright.

But the really exciting part of the pier was the mysterious region beneath it. Here was a nautical forest of piles and tie-beams whose bark was seashells and whose foliage was seaweed. The water was all round you; in bad weather it was like a caged menagerie of wild beasts which roared and hissed and came at you fiercely from behind the iron bars at your feet. An eerie green light added to the feeling of mystery, and an iron stairway plunging vertically downwards into the depths fathered strange fancies. Will never forgot the story someone had told him of a gentleman in a top-hat who came hand over hand up these stairs from out of the sea, and walked calmly away!

When at home, the boys would sometimes be taken to London on Saturdays by their father. The old knife-board horse bus started from the corner of Holloway Road, and on top of it the passengers sat in two rows, back to back. On either side of Charlie East, the driver, were a few seats for the " specials " who made the journey every day. Thomas Robinson was one of these, for he knew Charlie well, and his father, old East, who kept a livery and bait stables in Islington. Often on a slack Sunday he would arrange with the old man to take the family out for a drive to the country in his wagonette and stop for tea at some country inn.

Now he helped the boys up on to the high front seat beside Charlie. The conductor stood on a small step by the door at the back, which swung on its hinges like a street door. He issued no tickets, but the takings on these buses must have been satisfactory to the companies because for many years this was the general rule. When at last tickets were introduced, the conductors took it in bad part as an aspersion on their honesty!

Bus travel in London was far more exhilarating than it is today. Horses and horse-drawn vehicles filled the streets; heavy drays rumbled over the granite, landaus and victorias with smartly dressed women taking the air, shiny handsome cabs with little jingling bells, here and there a dogcart driven by a sporting youth in tweeds, milk carts, coal wagons, a young equestrian masher in a short drab overcoat, tight trousers and a flat hat, costers' carts filled with flowers and fruit, white-chapels, phætons, and even children's carts drawn by Shetland ponies. And, of course, many more buses, black with top-hatted gentlemen gravely reading their morning papers or perhaps discussing the Zulu War.

The prevalent odour was of horse, and Charlie had the air of one who dealt with living creatures, not with witless monsters of metal. Like Tony Weller, he ex-changed sallies with many a passing driver. There must be something in the business of passenger carrying which inspires repartee. The sedan-chair men in Stuart times were notorious for it, and Ned Ward gives some startling examples of verbal squibs among the Thames ferrymen. In the eighties the bus drivers knew every-thing and everybody; they would tip you a winner and whisper State secrets in your ear. Their wit was some-times extremely caustic. One driver who had been away for a few days on a cheap trip to Boulogne was cross-questioned about his experiences by a fare whom he particularly disliked. For some time he bore it in patience, but on being asked what had impressed him most while in France, replied gravely: " Hearing the bloody cocks crowing in French! "

The Robinsons' destination would be Danes Inn, where Thomas worked. In later years Heath remem-bered Fleet Street crowded with urchins who ran in and out among the horses gathering up the dung with brush and pan and the bewhiskered gentlemen in top-hats making for the chop houses which lined the streets.

Another and even greater treat was the Lord Mayor's Show. The family would assemble at Danes Inn, where

AN INTERESTING MOVEMENT TO BE INAUGURATED IN OUR PARKS
IN SPRING TO LIGHTLY TURN YOUNG MEN'S FANCIES TO THOUGHTS
OF INTELLECTUAL DEVELOPMENT

his mother would click her tongue at the dirty condition of the rooms and perhaps interview the charlady whose mind at the moment was engrossed with international affairs. She wanted to know why " them Zules (Zulus) was allowed to go on as they has." Then they went to a room which Thomas Robinson had hired—perhaps at " The George " in the Strand, which had windows over-looking the route. To the boys, keyed up to a high pitch of expectation, it always seemed a never-ending wait, despite the excitement of watching the huge, gathering crowd.

In those days Temple Bar stood astride the Strand and Fleet Street, while the Law Courts were a forest of scaffolding. The show was always a thing of wonder, and each one had its particular thrill. One year the procession, which was under the management of George Sanger, included a car representing the British Empire. On a tall pedestal stood a stately lady dressed as Britan-nia, and at her feet were others figuring as the colonies and possessions.

As the procession moved westward from the City, it was evident to the onlookers that Britannia and her pedestal were too lofty to clear the Bar. The Robinsons held their breath; then down jumped one of the colonies, winding a handle behind the car he lowered Britannia in true Heath Robinson fashion to a safe level. Having passed the Bar, he wound her up again to her former elevated position and she passed majestic-ally on her way. The boys thought it was very much like the penny steamers on the Thames which lowered their funnels on reaching a bridge !

Being theatrical producers themselves, they enjoyed pageantry and stage performances with critical relish. Sometimes they were taken for a treat to the Standard Theatre in Hoxton, which seated 4,500 people and was one of the biggest theatres in London; or to see George

Conquest at the Eagle in the City Road; other times it would be Hengler's Circus or the Mohawk Minstrels.

But they preferred theatres, and especially the Eagle, since this meant the added thrill of staying the night with relations who kept a pub in Whitechapel. This was long before the days of early closing, and late at night when the boys came from the theatre, conviviality would be at its height. The gas-lit bar with its ornate mirrors and shiny counters, the high-complexioned ladies who presided over the bewildering assortment of bottles, the noisy, bowler-hatted customers and the torrid alcoholic sunshine all combined to make it seem more dreamlike than the stage.

CHAPTER VI

THE DEAD HAND OF TRADITION

THERE was never much doubt about the profession Heath Robinson was to take up. His father and his Uncle Charles were artists, his two brothers, Tom and Charles, had decided to become artists, so it was not surprising that he should follow his natural bent and become an artist, too. He had no leanings towards business, and although he had shown no unusual talent for drawing, there was nothing else that he wished to do more. Indeed, when at the age of fifteen he went to the Islington Art School and mixed with other young students he soon developed majestic ambitions.

The wine of youth is corked if it has no sparkling dreams of the future; men who have never looked forward with fantastic hope have never been young at all. Will was not conceited, and he did not exactly picture himself as a Great Man; but, as he himself put it, he flattered himself with the possibilities rather than the probabilities of what awaited him in the future. Having digested the lives of the Old Masters, he saw himself painting frescoes in monasteries, or perhaps decorating some lofty chapel roof in the manner of Michelangelo, afterwards nonchalantly watching the crowds of admiring critics lying flat on their backs and peering at his work through opera glasses. At other times he saw himself a romantic cosmopolitan wanderer, painting mountain scenery and ancient cities in the grand manner and only occasionally visiting his native England.

Tom and Charles were just as ambitious, and so great was to be their impact on the world of Art that it seemed necessary to define the province of each of the trio so as to avoid overlapping and confusion.

" Tom," wrote Heath Robinson, " as a kind of artistic cock of the walk took upon himself the rôle of Michelangelo. Charles and I had to be content with those of Raphael and Titian respectively. After a while, with the full approval of the committee of three I altered my rôle to that of a follower of Claude and Turner."*

But even these generous limitations soon became irksome; so presently Tom would be painting an occasional landscape and Will would keep his hand in with a sketch of some terrific theme such as " Creation," " The Last Judgment," or " The Triumph of Order over Chaos," while Charles, who was apprenticed to a lithographer was equally happy in either of these rôles, or indeed in any other. From these giddy heights it was a little tame to descend to the mundane and unimaginative exercises of the Islington Art School.

At that time Art was heavily dominated by the classical tradition, and line drawing was regarded as mere " sketching "—no more than a preliminary to finished paintings. The public looked for living truth and idealism to the Royal Academy, whose walls had for many years become a sort of Illustrated Summer Number in colours. On the one hand, there were paltry subjects sentimentally treated, on the other, solemn and deadly dull pictures of a prim decorative school which worked archaically with a thinly disguised affectation of naïveté. There had already been a revolt against these forests of banality—the Æsthetic movement of the eighties; but its camp followers, the soulful young women and the precious youths, were such an easy butt

* *My Line of Life*, by W. Heath Robinson (Blackie).

for the satirists that people soon began to laugh at them. Gilbert's " Greenery-yallery, Grosvenor Gallery young man " and du Maurier's Mrs. Cimabue Browne and other earnest young ladies lionizing some long-haired æsthete reassured the public that all this searching for beauty was mere pose, and that the Royal Academy was as safe a guide to artistic taste as the Bank of England was for sound financial policy.

When Latin and even Greek were sonorously quoted in the House of Commons to add weight to specious political pronouncements, it was natural that artists should look to Rome and Athens. So Alma Tadema's marbles were much admired and a host of sedulous imitators decorated the gardens of suburbia and the bedrom walls of Kensington with facsimiles of classic figures clothed in chiton and peplum. Slavish reproduction of petty details at the expense of clear and broad conceptions, reduced much of the official sculpture to the level of tailors' dummies.

Classic statuary is cold, uncomforting stuff for an emotional generation and something else had to be found to warm the blood. So the artists turned to senti-mental abstractions from everyday life; well-behaved children exhibiting the Christian virtues, women ideal-ized to the point of apotheosis, soldiers performing in-credible feats of heroism, and so on. These appeals to crude emotion were entirely divorced from any notion of individual insight, subtlety of presentation, or artistic style. No demands were made on the spectator. The best picture was that which told a story in the plainest possible words, and the ultimate goal was not far removed from photography in colours.

With such an outlook the high priests of orthodox art cast a disparaging eye on the black and white artist. The splendid work which was being done by such men as Charles Keene, Linley Sambourne, George Pinwell,

Frederick Sandys and Arthur Boyd Houghton was ignored by the official arbitrators of taste as being not " serious work." Anything humorous came especially under this ban, and Phil May was not elected to the Royal Academy, although he was proposed by Lord Leighton, the president.

Training in nearly all the art schools was entirely in keeping with these archaic ideas. In most cases originality in the students was excised by severely academic training and by hard and fast courses of instruction which tried to suppress anything that contradicted the shibboleths of bygone teachers. The Academy schools insisted on the students who applied for admission passing a test which ignored creative imagination and the grasp of colour and form, but demanded skill in niggling and stippling surfaces laboriously copied from the antique.

" The great and golden rule of art," wrote William Blake, " as well as of life, is this : that the more distinct, sharp and wiry the bounding line, the more perfect the work of art; and the less keen and sharp, the greater is the evidence of weak imitation, plagiarism, and bungling."*

Most of the art schools in the eighties could hardly have agreed with him less. Lines they regarded as positive defects, and the medium most favoured was the " stump " for smearing on the powdered chalk, which is really only suitable for the representation of surfaces. Except at the Slade School, where Legros was teaching, no constructive drawing was to be found. For the epoch-making work in black and white which flourished towards the end of the century, official teaching could claim no credit whatever.

The school at which the Robinson brothers studied was very much in the chip and plaster tradition, and it

* Gilchrist, II, 162.

must have resembled a decayed museum with its miscellany of classical fragments. There were plaster casts of the Venus de Medici, the Discobolus and the Roman Emperors. Dismembered pieces of male and female anatomy hung on the walls; there were odd bits of ornament, mutilated human trunks, amputated hands and feet. The students lived in a limbo of plaster corpses, and they became so used to drawing fragments that they could hardly imagine a complete figure. To carry things a little further away from reality, the plaster, being unwashable, was painted at intervals to restore its whiteness, and thereby much of the modelling was obliterated.

Looking back on those days, Heath was surprised to remember the marvellous enthusiasm with which he and many of his fellow students stuck to these quaint exercises, and even to the drawing of cubes, cones and vases arranged on boards. Too much plaster copied over the years deadens the creative faculty and plodding persistency is all that remains. Most of us have seen examples of those solid tributes to the Muses which inspired such artists—the Victorian paintings of still life : succulent studies of sirloins and vegetables, oil paintings of dahlias and peonies arranged as if for a flower show.

Heath Robinson long remembered one devoted follower of this tradition who in spite of his utmost efforts would frequently fall asleep, exhausted by the dullness of his subjects. And, not unlike him, was an elderly ex-civil servant, who, on retiring, bravely decided to start a new profession and become an artist. In spite of a bald head and a drooping moustache, he was as simple and eager as a child.

Another student was a lady who, at the age of fifty, suddenly felt that she had missed her vocation, and gave up music, at which she had already spent most of her life and won considerable success. Tough and determined as ever, with an explosion of grey hair crowning her bony head, she worked so hard that she often had to bathe her eyes in an eye bath to relieve the strain.

More formidable was an old sea captain, who put in a day or two at the school whenever his ship dropped anchor in the Port of London. A dour man, the high spirits of the younger students irritated him so much that he could only work in a small private room, where he made laborious copies in oils of a book of views of the Isle of Wight in the best pavement manner.

The art mistress of the school, Miss Thomson, although not at all a formidable woman, was able to exercise authority and win respect. A little simple and unsophisticated, she believed implicitly in her school, and everyone liked her. She also took the master of the school at his face value, which is more than some of the students did. These were times when Great Men, or those who imagined themselves such, dressed and played the part. But Henri Bosdet must have overplayed it a little, or possibly his French descent told against him. Miss Thomson was romantically affected by his long, silky beard and his wavy hair, and overawed by his exquisite clothes. Who could doubt that a man who wore such a beautiful black velvet coat and smart-bow-tie, and who surveyed the work of the students with such mannered elegance through his gold-rimmed monocle was a very great artist indeed? The students suspected otherwise, and as if to emphasize their difference in nationality addressed him stolidly, and to his great annoyance, as " Mister Bozzdett."

Years later, when Heath Robinson was married and living at Cranleigh, and dressed in his oldest clothes was trundling a barrow across his front lawn, an elegant apparition not unlike M. Bosdet appeared suddenly at the gate. He wore a grey coat exquisitely cut to show the delicate outline of his figure, and his beautifully shaped legs were shown off to advantage in black velvet knee-breeches. A wide black hat reposed upon his long hair. Before the master of the house could recover from his astonishment the visitor handed him a card bearing the inscription "M. Renée de Boudoir," and said: "Will you take this to your master, my good man?"

What followed was typical of Heath Robinson. Bowing politely, he went indoors, changed and washed, and returned to greet his visitor. If M. de Boudoir suspected that he had committed a gaffe, he was far too much a man of the world to acknowledge it.

The Islington Art School was one of the many "prep. schools" for the schools of the Royal Academy. The scales on which entrants for these last were weighed were rusty and worn in the extreme, and it is probable that anyone who showed any real traces of originality would be ploughed. What was looked for in the student was a capacity for laboured perfection of execution and for slavish imitation of the Old Masters. Many promising young artists were turned down again and again and only about one in five ever gained admittance. Some of them gave up in despair and took to another calling; a few had the courage to stick to it and strike out a line of their own without any academic training at all. Heath was lucky enough to pass the test at his second attempt. He exchanged plaster for marble and the breezy art room in Islington for the solemn halls of the British and Natural History museums.

A fellow student who remained one of his closest friends in adult life remembers his first meeting with him a little time before this. One day he was idly strolling about an empty room in the Natural History Museum when a wild-looking, shockheaded youth appeared at the door, evidently meaning to enter, but

H.R.—C*

vanished on seeing another man. Each knew the other by sight but for some time they were too shy to face the embarrassment of speaking to one another. At length the ice was broken and they sat together at the school lectures. Both of them would have much preferred to mix with the others and enjoy the sardonic wit of Sims and other heroes, but bashfulness prevented it. In Heath's case this shyness lasted all his life.

The British Museum, with its chilly silences and its frowning statues of gods and heroes, is hardly a cheerful place, and lest a jarring note should be struck the students were expected to conduct themselves with a seemly gravity. However, one day Heath Robinson, returning from his work, gaily whistling " Little Dolly Daydream," rounded a statue and walked slap into the Chief Librarian. This was sacrilege and there was nearly serious trouble over it. The incident was described in verse by a fellow student, George Hering:

" Of all the students of the Greek Antiquities
    The best behaved was Robinson, a youth
Who, working hard, avoiding all iniquities
    Pursued, with earnest searching after truth,
His aim, which was (if he don't think it bad o' me
    To tell it you) obtaining if he could
Admission to the schools of the Academy
    Nor can one say his purpose was not good.

He, being hungry, went one day to lunch
    A frugal meal of cocoa and a bun
Which 'twas his daily wont to sip and munch
    Approximately at the hour of One.
His hunger being satisfied, he traced
    His steps to work again without delay
For he was one who would not wish to waste
    In brutal gluttony his time away.

His face was glad. His drawing had progressed
Amazing well of late and he, content
In the possession of a mind at rest
Tripped gaily onward, whistling as he went
All unconcerned he whistled as he went
Nor knew it was the Chief Librarian
Who stood, as on a catalogue intent.
Alas! unwary 'un
Will no one warn him of the dreadful doom
That like Damocles' sword o'er him doth wait?
Into the second Greco-Roman room
He enters, whistling still—and meets his fate!

But fate is kind, pours oil upon the storm,
For Bamlett*, like an angel from the skies
Places betwixt the twain his god-like form—
Intreats, implores, with many tears and sighs
That for this once the crime may be forgiven;
Brings evidence to show that otherwise
The lad was good and up till now has striven
To do in all the proper thing and right
Is also sure he will apologize
When he has quite recovered from his fright.

Slowly and by degrees the day is gained
Peace is proclaimed and ere the fall of night
It is announced that though his name be stained
For ever, with a blot that will not fade
Though he has done a heinous deadly thing
Though he has e'en a bye-law disobeyed
For once the hand of Justice will be stayed
For once the trampled serpent shall not sting! "

Will had been drawing antiques since he was fifteen
and he was dismayed to discover on entering the

* The Custodian of the Elgin Room, a short, fat man.

academy art schools that he was expected to continue doing so; it was only occasionally that his studies were varied by painting or drawing from life.

First you had to enter for a probationary exam. If this was passed successfully, two more " antique " chalk drawings had to be made and passed by the examiner before you were allowed to go into the " middle school " where you did another two antique studies, this time in monochrome.

Yet once again he was struck by the extraordinary enthusiasm of many of his fellow students. There was one young lady who had worked so diligently to improve her stippling that it resembled the finest crochet work. Another student, a candidate for admission to the R.A. schools, who earned his living in an office, was so hard put to it that he could only spare a quarter of an hour a day for copying his antiques. Rushing into the museum he would set up his easel as if it were a military exercise and paint frantically with one eye on his watch. In this way it took him many months to finish a drawing. Some years after he had left the school, Heath Robinson found him busily painting a sunset not far from London. Three years later he saw him again, at work on the same painting which had evidently been done in the same brief, disjointed manner. Cheerful and indomitable to the last, he was still at work on the picture when he fell ill and died.

With such ardent material to work upon even the Royal Academy art schools were able to preserve their ancient methods intact without a revolt from within. Heath Robinson thought they could scarcely have altered since the days of the Academy's founder, and he imagined the ghost of Sir Joshua Reynolds stalking through the studios or the great yard at the side of Burlington House with a volume of the Discourses under his arm.

He thought that he gained little or nothing from the tedious years he spent under Sir Joshua's shadow, but it is quite possible that his creative faculty was strengthened by being frustrated. Art must keep on the move or it will fossilize. In the eighties the petrification of official Art had grown so thick that only genuine originality and real force of talent could pierce it. The weaklings were stifled under the hard crust, but a brilliant band of rebels with such men as Phil May, Sime and Beardsley in the vanguard, were thrusting up from beneath and blossoming in a renaissance of black and white drawing, with new methods of reproduction to help them.

CHAPTER VII

THE THREE MUSKETEERS

THE outlook of young art students may vary a little from generation to generation, but fundamentally it is always the same in its carefree exuberance and its happy feeling of release from the shackles of convention. Other young men will be caught up in the cogs of the Machine, or strangled by the tabus of polite society; they will have to toe the line and be branded with the mark of the Herd. But an artist is a joyous rebel who can dress as he likes, behave as he likes, and lead where others are forced to follow.

Heath Robinson and his brothers were much like other young artists of the nineties in their outlook. Though they were not priggish about it, they were a little sorry for the young fellows in other walks of life. They affected rather a picturesque attire, wearing black cloaks and broad-brimmed hats. Charles suggested the Quartier Latin. The least pronounced in the eccentricity of his dress was Heath, who was also the shyest. At that time he was regarded by nearly everyone he met as a very serious young man who held himself aloof from the rowdiness of Bohemia. But he was not aloof from choice: he found it impossible to share his highly coloured imagination with others, and so it remained unexpressed and found vent in daydreams.

He was not at all mercenary and rather prided himself upon it. One day he picked up a half sovereign in Chancery Lane. He was elated over his luck, but a little later, when Tom congratulated him, he owned that it had cost him an extra sovereign among his friends, who insisted on celebrating his good luck in the only way they considered suitable! If money and fame came his way, he would accept them with easy grace. Even the Old Masters had done this. There could be no harm in taking the gifts of the gods once you had seen through the hollowness of temporal values. But meanwhile Tom and Charles were earning their living, and his parents were finding it hard to pay him his allowance. He saw that he must come down to earth and do something practical. Giving up for the moment his plans for painting the Himalayas or a Benedictine chapel roof, he decided to paint Hampstead Heath; for as he told himself, this had the solid advantage of being within walking distance of his home, now in Stroud Green.

Years later he told a friend that he could hardly bear to revisit this early sketching ground, so sadly changed did he find it. Hampstead Lane, which is now a roaring motorway, was then a charming country lane. No unmannerly suburbs sprawled across the middle distance: sunlit fields with mellow red farm buildings spread towards Harrow and Finchley. In the Vale of Health the afternoon sun shone through the pollarded willows onto a gay crowd of holidaymakers, and in the shade were rustic wooden tables at which people were served with tea. From the roundabouts came the shrill cries of children and the cheerful lilt of " The Man who Broke the Bank of Monte Carlo," or " A Bicycle Made for Two." Near Caen's dark recesses badgers were still to be found, and nightingales sang in Bishop's Wood. You could still see Constable's knoll of Scotch firs, and rough sandy paths led to the " Bull and Bush," where you could order a brew of the famous barley wine.

Here Heath Robinson spent the best part of a summer, painting industriously and thoroughly enjoying himself. For company he had assorted members of the Undeserving Poor who in those days were not troubled by unwelcome attentions from a Ministry of Labour. Reclining on the grass beside him they would engage him in easy conversation. How they lived was a mystery. Perhaps, he thought, they were thieves, but if so they made no attempts to steal his paints and canvases which lay within easy reach. It was also a mystery how some of the other artists on Hampstead Heath supported themselves. One of them was an elderly Scotsman who sold his pictures at junkshop prices to meet his bills, and another was a condescending but decayed doctor who, for some reason, had lost his practice.

At the end of the summer Heath picked out the best of his paintings and took them to a shop in the Balls Pond Road. The dealer, a bald, friendly man, looked at them for a long time through half closed eyes with his head on one side. Every freelance knows this dreadful moment. The embryo writer suddenly realizes that the man sitting beside him on a bus is reading his first humorous story in *London Opinion* and nervously waits for a chuckle—but hears only a dyspeptic sniff; the young musician plays his first composition at the sitting-room piano and looks anxiously round at his audience—and sees them looking like toy rubber pigs.

At last the dealer inquired how long he had been painting, and Will replied, about four or five years. Asked whether he had ever sold a painting, he said no. The dealer then wanted to know if he had to depend upon his earnings for a living, and on hearing how matters stood said kindly: " Well, in that case I should try something else." After helping him tie up his pictures he shook hands with him in a most friendly way and stood at the door watching him as he walked away. The only possible consolation was the reflection that a man who lived in the Balls Pond Road could not possibly know anything about Art!

The only painting he sold out of all those he did on the Heath was bought by his old friend, Mrs. Bernard Smith, and it was impossible not to suspect that she bought it more from kindliness than from an appreciation of its merit. At any rate, it enabled the young painter to take a holiday in Cornwall with Fred Smith; and looking back on this holiday in later years he felt that he had never been paid so generously.

But when the holiday came to an end it became necessary to consider his future more seriously. Landscape painting evidently held out no prospects; what else was there he could do? Charles's apprenticeship to the lithographer had come to an end some time ago and he was beginning to make a name for himself as a delicate black and white artist. He had illustrated Robert Louis Stevenson's *A Child's Book of Verses* and he was doing well with some of the magazines. Tom was soon to illustrate *The Sentimental Journey,* published by Bliss, Sands, and he had been commissioned to do the drawings for that famous series of articles on London life by George R. Sime, in the *Strand Magazine.* Perhaps, thought Heath, he could become an illustrator, too.

As a child his slate had been almost a second mother tongue, to describe small adventures and to express the workings of his imagination. Later, in boyhood, all three brothers had used their sketch books in much the same way—as a writer uses his notebook, or as a professor of science uses the cuff of his dress shirt. It was these sketches, made over the years and without any ulterior aim but just for the fun of it, which sowed the seeds of his career. The turgid, pontifical instruction he had received at the Royal Academy Art School had no effect on him at all, except perhaps to strengthen his determination to break away from the dead hand of ancestor worship and strike out a line of his own.

The moment was an especially favourable one for a black and white artist, since between the years 1880 and 1891 experiments had been made in mechanical reproduction which gave the death blow to wood engraving.

Before the invention of photographic methods, and in spite of such men as Bewick, the unhappy artist was restricted by the conventions of the engraver and much of his originality was smothered. He could not draw as he wished; he could only draw what this cumbersome method was able to reproduce. And even within these limits, unless he had the collaboration of a highly skilled engraver who was in sympathy with his work, much of the feeling which he put into his drawing was ironed out. Except for a few autocrats like Meissonier, artists felt obliged to draw always with the thought of the engraver uppermost in their minds.

What happened in earlier days to men who disregarded the wood engravers is shown by the trying experience of Dante Gabriel Rossetti.

" I have designed five blocks for Tennyson," he wrote to W. Bell Scott, " save seven which are still cutting and maiming. It is a thankless task. After a fortnight's work my block goes to the engraver, like Agag, delicately, and is hewn in pieces before the Lord Harry."

And to ease his ruffled feelings he composed some verses to the Dalziel Brothers, the engravers:

" O woodman spare that block
A gash not anyhow!
It took ten days by clock
I'd fain protect it now.
Chorus—
Wild laughter from Dalziel's workshop."

Rosetti grew exasperated with Dalziel, and Dalziel was certainly exasperated with him. Blocks flew backwards and forwards with angry letters. The poor publisher, Mr. Moxon, pleaded, interceded, and finally died of worry.

By the new zincographic methods better results were obtained more cheaply and in much less time. There was no need for an artist to hamper himself with the impediments of wood engraving. He drew as he pleased, on paper, and his drawing was photographed in reverse on to a zinc plate covered with a sensitized film of gelatine. His lines were protected against the acid, which was applied to eat away the rest of the plate's surface, leaving the lines raised in relief. When inked they could be used for printing.

This revolution in method produced a spate of new illustrated books, papers and magazines, and artists found themselves in great demand. At first they scarcely realized what they could do with the new process, but soon they found that they could draw with freedom and that their work was not distorted when it appeared in print. Prices for work improved, and more and more artists turned to illustration work. Thirty years had passed since the last great efflorescence of line illustration, and now another and greater one had begun.

Heath Robinson went to work in his father's studio in Danes Inn, off the Strand. Thomas Robinson, still working for the *Penny Illustrated*, had a couple of rooms at the top of Number One. The place was rather like a prison. You went up a wide circular stairway with an iron railing to protect you from sudden death, and a smell of ancient dinners mingled with the odour of musty stone came at you in gusts. A friend of Will's who lived there remembers sharing a groundfloor flat with a young solicitor who dressed with care, wore a monocle, and spoke at Conservative meetings where he belauded his own side and vilified the other with equal disregard for the truth. But he lived a double life, for he kept potatoes in his bath, and in his sideboard there were usually pigs' jaws and the remains of Bath chaps which he was saving for soup. When invited out to dinner he would fast so that he might do greater justice to his friends' hospitality. On the opposite side lived a man who wrote hymn tunes and music for comic operas; when he wanted food he blew a bugle out of the window and shouted for it!

Mr. Robinson's rooms bore evidence of neglect and bachelor discomfort. On the mantelshelf was a dusty and dilapidated model of a ship; the walls were decorated with some old charts, a blunderbuss and an ancient allegorical print of the " Spirit of Gout," which seemed to have strayed from some doctor's waiting room. Still more macabre was the desiccated corpse of a cat which hung by the fireplace.

Tom and Charles had already been working there for some time, helped by their father's knowledge of the world. Although neither of them ever said so, they must have thought him a little oldfashioned for such lively and progressive young fellows as themselves who belonged to the New Movement in Art.

With his bold drawings in the famous *Yellow Book,* of which he was joint editor with Henry Harland, Beardsley was soon to touch off a " boom in yellow." The *Yellow Book* caused a sensation; it was considered startling, repellent, fascinating, or shocking; though John Lane, the publisher, did his best to keep the irrepressible Beardsley under control and to lower the temperature of the journal with injections of staid literature and prim pictures by members of the Royal Academy, it was a little too much for the stilted conventions of those days; and Beardsley, a thin, delicate figure with superabundant energy, was to die of consumption at the age of twenty-five. Oscar Wilde described him as having "a face like a silver hatchet, with grass-green hair." Like Picasso he was vehemently lauded and scorned, but unlike him he was very susceptible to praise or criticism. When Whistler, won round at last, told him that he had made a great mistake and that he was a very great artist, he burst into tears.

With his freakish, irresponsible spirit of fun, Beardsley did a great deal to break down the conventional Victorian idea of humour and the niggling tradition of fussy detail. His fine sweeping line and his bold masses of black, coupled with a daring originality of design, was something new, and his impact on artists was very great.

Sime, who became editor of *The Idler* and *Eureka*, had a highly developed sense of the ridiculous and he tilted at Victorian smugness and respectability. His methods were all his own and, like Beardsley, he owed nothing to academic training. Indeed, it is hardly possible to imagine him with his fantastic, dreamlike fancy spending years of his life in the dreary temples of orthodoxy.

Heath Robinson was influenced a good deal by both these men, for he, too, was inspired far more by his imagination than by the prospect of mere graphic reporting, and he also came under the influence of Walter Crane and Kate Greenaway. At Danes Inn he worked hard, and at last, choosing some of the best of his collection of drawings, set out to assail the editors and the publishers. In these days a young artist who wished to make an impression on a publisher would wear a top-hat. Whether Will wore one is not remembered, but it is considered that he was desperate enough to miss no chance which might further his prospects.

This is a most trying time for a young artist, for there is no concealing the portfolio in which you carry your

pictures; everyone seems to be looking at you, ready
to smile a little scornfully at your impudence. The
tedious delay in the waiting-room, where perhaps competitors eye you askance, seems to last for hours, until as
in a dentist's waiting-room you are tempted to run away.
Even more trying is the awful moment when the editor
looks at your drawings with a carefully non-committal
expression; and when he turns them down with the
polite anodyne that he will always be pleased to see any
further work of yours, you give him a sickly smile and try
hard to look as if you believed him.

Heath tried his luck vainly with John Lane in Vigo
Street and Grant Richards in Leicester Square. Heine-
mann and Dent were at first no more encouraging,
though in the outer office of the last firm he met a young
man named Frank Swinnerton, with whom he became
very friendly.

However, writing of him a little later on, Mr. Swinnerton says : " They (the Robinson brothers) were
working together on a book or books for J. M. Dent. . . .
Charles was drawing balloony babies, and they may
have taken a joint hand in three books by William
Canton. They used to swing into the Dent shop at
29-30 Bedford Street like the three musketeers. My
memory is of Tom, rather small and sedate, first; Will,
very thin and taller than the others, in an overcoat
which was so closely buttoned that he looked thinner
than ever, in the middle; and Charles, always freer and
more jaunty in his movements than the others, last.

" They would stand talking with me while they
waited until Mr. Dent could see them, and then they
filed upstairs. What happened then I don't know; but
soon afterwards they would come clattering down again
like schoolboys, always very much amused at what had
happened above.

" One day one of them (I think Will) told me that

J. M. D. had patted them on the shoulders and said:
' I am proud of you, boys! ' He was not paying very
much for their drawings. My belief is that he rated
Tom more highly than the others, and after a time I
fancy Charles was the only one of the team to come in."

Some time before this Will's spell of beginner's
failure had been broken, first by selling a picture to the
firm of Cassell and then by having some drawings published in *Good Words*. This journal was one of the very
few which aimed at a high standard of black and white
illustration; the editor was sympathetic to his artists and
he was almost the only one who gave detailed mention
of their work in a complete index to each volume. Such
consideration for artists was almost unheard of in those
days and *Good Words* attracted some of the best of
them, including Linley Sambourne and Harry Furniss.

Heath was elated at this piece of luck and was able to
bear with more courage his inevitable early failures.
Then another success came to him which, viewed in
retrospect, must have seemed absurd but which at the
time was probably magnified out of all proportion. In
those days there were firms such as Partridge's which
gave the blocks they had used a sort of St. Luke's Summer of commercial utility by selling them in the secondhand market. After the transaction, hack artists were
employed to adapt them, possibly for some quite different use. Thus the heroine of a story might be lifted out
of her romantic preoccupation with the hero and find
herself advertising the sale of soap or some other useful
commodity.

The commission which came to him was to alter one
of these " clichés," as they were called. He had to adapt
a drawing of some fishes from a book on natural history
so that it could be used to illustrate a fairy story. This
was done by painting over the indication numbers and
introducing a " water baby." As he wrote later, " It

certainly appeared to be economical for I suppose they only had to pay for the baby, the price for which was not high although the baby was a fat one. The fishes, if they had to be paid for at all, they could have had at secondhand rates."*

* *My Line of Life.*

CHAPTER VIII

THE GOLDEN AGE OF ILLUSTRATION

THE studios and methods of young artists vary almost as much as their work. Charles Keene's first studio was a rickety attic in the Strand, full of old costumes, armour, books and crockery, a hammock slung across the cobwebbed rafters, and an ancient ship's stove for a fire. Beardsley worked in elegant seclusion and disliked anyone in his room when he was drawing. Phil May drew just anywhere—on the backs of menu cards, in bed, or out in the street. Pellegrini boasted that he had no sketchbooks at all, declaring that he kept his impressions in his head, but on his death it was found that he had done a great many drawings at public dinners—on his shirtfronts which he carefully preserved from the wash!

Heath Robinson's first studio, which he shared with Billinghurst, was a small jerry-built room in Howland Street off the Tottenham Court Road. It had no windows, but only a skylight, and their Jewish landlady let it to them cheaply, aware no doubt that the rentable value was somewhat diminished by a powerful equine odour which filtered up through the floorboards from the stable below. The two young men endured these discomforts for several months but were at last obliged to move to Gower Street.

Here, perched on the roof of a house, they found a flimsily built erection which was more like an early airship than a studio. It was icy-cold in winter and in summer like a furnace. But the bones of the sea-loving Robinson ancestors stirred in Will when storms were blowing and the studio rocked like a ship on high seas. Sometimes his lively fancy saw the two of them airborne over London, pancaking on Bedford Street to compel some stubborn publisher to grant them a fabulous commission.

Billinghurst had begun his training at the Barnsbury Art School, and he entered the Academy schools at about the same time as Heath. Though his temperament was very different from theirs, all the Robinsons were fond of him. He was cautious and in delicate health, and having developed a technique for animal drawings he stuck to it and never tried anything else. Before many years his health grew worse and he died.

One of the first successes in books which came to Heath Robinson was a commission to illustrate a series of Indian tales collected by Dr. W. H. D. Rouse and published by Nutt under the title of *The Giant Crab*.

Although at this time his technique was immature, his imagination found plenty of scope in the commission, and his drawings of animals showed how keenly he could observe. Dr. Rouse liked his work. In 1941 Heath wrote to him: " I remember how encouraged I was by your appreciation of my illustrations in the book, and in those days encouragement was specially valuable to me. I remember, too, how much I enjoyed the work. The stories seemed to suit me exactly, as they would now. I often wish I had to illustrate them all over again, but this time with bright colours. They gave me such free play for using that fancy I love to exercise as few other subjects have done.

" Not so happy is the work I am now engaged upon— making fun of the enemy, as I did throughout the last war. . . . I have heard on one or two occasions that my

"MASTER PETER," FROM *DON QUIXOTE*
—Courtesy of J. M. Dent & Sons

war drawings have been taken by them as quite serious propositions."

In the same year, 1897, he did sixteen illustrations for an edition of *Don Quixote,* twenty-four drawings for *Pilgrim's Progress,* and sixteen for Hans Andersen's *Danish Fairy Tales and Legends,* all published by Bliss, Sands. Two years later he illustrated Hans Andersen again, with his two brothers, and *The Talking Thrush,* by Dr. Rouse, both published by Dent; he also did some 130 drawings for *The Arabian Nights,* published by Constable.

Some young artists, especially those who are to die young, have an extraordinary precocity which launches them fully fledged, as if fate were willing to waive the apprenticeship in compensation for their short careers. Others develop more slowly; but however slowly they develop there are usually signs of what is to come which is apparent to enterprising publishers who are on the lookout for young artists of promise. When Dana Gibson was at the beginning of his career he was told that his drapery was like sheets of boiler metal; all the same, the editor who said this encouraged him because he saw that he had the makings of a great artist. In the eighties, Heath Robinson's drapery was often rather like metal sheets and his wide-eyed children were sometimes very wooden indeed. There was no remarkable sureness of touch; nevertheless, discerning men could see something unusual in his work, especially his whimsical illustrations of fairy tales.

Illustrating books for children is not easy work because children are sharp and merciless critics. They demand very definite and objective treatment of subjects and they are quick to notice flaws which arise from the artist's vagueness of conception. They expect to be taken to real fairylands and not mere suburbia of the adult world. A successful fairy-tale artist must believe

FROM *THE BELLS*, BY EDGAR ALLAN POE
—Courtesy of George Bell & Sons

in his pictures. Above all, he must not be condescending. He must see things from a child's point of view, which means that he must have a heart eternally young. His illustrations should make you believe that there really are enchanted isles far removed from the commonplace world in which we live, and that he has been there and knows all about them.

This is where the " fey " side of Heath Robinson stood him in good stead. He never talked down to a child and no matter what extravaganza he drew he always seemed to take it seriously. It was about this time that he began drawing absurdities especially to amuse the children he met. One is reminded of young Edward Lear in the gigantic mansion of the Earl of Derby—Lear who caused such roars of merriment below stairs that the astonished earl inquired what was happening, and on hearing the explanation gave orders that the eccentric tutor was henceforth to take his meals with the rest of the family.

Heath Robinson, when he was amusing children, did not compose limericks and illustrate them, but he drew quaint old men with immensely tall, lidded hats out of which fledglings peeped. This was very much like Lear's old man in the limerick whose beard was a nesting place for a whole aviary. Like Lear, Heath saw things from a very strange angle, which he justified with perfect gravity and impeccable logic, almost compelling you to do violence to your reason. The spectator, in fact, found himself looking at the world through eyes which were not quite human.

In 1900 he illustrated an Edgar Allan Poe volume in Bell's " Endymion " series of poets. This was hardly the sort of task you would expect such a man to undertake, and it is strange, perhaps, that he should have responded to these peculiar poems at all. They reach out into a sombre Unknown. To translate them the artist must needs have been in a similar mood of emotional cognition to that in which they were written. Something of their subtle meaning he certainly felt, something of their music he caught in harmonious line. But how deeply he penetrated into the heart of them is another matter. Only an artist cast in the same psychological mould as Poe could have succeeded fully.

Two years later were published no less than five books illustrated by Heath Robinson, and a comparison of these books with his earlier illustrations shows not only the inequality of his work at this time but how quickly he was advancing.

In the first of these, *Don Quixote* (Dent), his drawings are far and away superior to those of his previous attempt. Not nearly so good are his illustrations of Professor Schück's *Mediæval Stories,* which are much more stilted and lifeless. On the other hand, his vignettes and coloured pictures for Roland Carse's *Monarchs of Merry England* are much more in the style of his comic advertising work. The doggerel could have been no inspiration to his more subtle vein of humour, and all one can say is that his illustrations are appropriate to the so-called humour of potted history. Poor, too, in comparison with his marvellous illustrations of Shakespeare which came later are his sixteen drawings for *Lamb's Tales from Shakespeare,* published by Sands. The harsh lines, heavy cross hatching and lack of balance are all rather apparent, and both Ariel and Titania are lay figures compared with the faery creatures which he learned to draw when his technique was more developed.

As he gained skill and confidence, Heath began to experience the special difficulties of illustrators who happen to be artists of originality. His opinion was that illustrations for books should never perforce be too literal and that artists should be given the same freedom of expression as musical composers working out a theme. Like most men who are more than mere plumbers in Art, he disliked taking orders. Perfect sympathy between author and artist is as rare as it is in marriage. For true harmony of collaboration the artist must feel things in the same way as the writer whose book he illustrates. Failing this, he may do his conscientious best to interpret without inspiration, or follow his own inspiration which may have little or no connection with what has been written.

Although whenever he undertook a commission to illustrate a book Heath Robinson did his best to keep the author's description in mind, he was too individual an artist to be satisfied with a mere pictorial restatement of the facts. His drawing as it developed became contrapuntal to the written theme, enriching but not re-echoing it.

But even with such freedom as this—freedom which was never grudged by authors or publishers—he chafed under the restraint, and most probably he regarded other men's writings as nothing but an irksome restraint on his imagination. So although never posing as a literary man he began to feel the urge to become his own author. Once again, therefore, he branched off on a new but quite unpretentious line of fantasy, writing and illustrating a book for children which he called *Uncle Lubin*.

CHAPTER IX

UNCLE LUBIN PULLS THE STRINGS

IT would be interesting if more artists had left us descriptions of their muses. Those of the Flemish School must have been wonderfully consoling in moments of depression—far more so than the frigid and virtuous ladies who inspired the Royal Academicians of the nineties. Doré's was not the sort of muse one would care to meet on a dark night, and Goya's must have been even more terrifying. As for the muses of the Cubists, the Vorticists and the Surrealists, they hardly bear thinking about.

Heath Robinson's muse, Uncle Lubin, was a queer little creature with a tall hat secured by a chin-ribbon tied in a bow, and a belted greatcoat reaching down to his long, narrow boots.

"At one time in his existence," Heath wrote, " he must have wandered long in Alice's Wonderland. The only book he seems to have read was Gilbert's *Bab Ballads,* but even these he did not read as we read them; he took them quite seriously as we do Shakespeare and Smiles's *Self Help* and *Eric, or Little by Little.* He was sincerity itself, and he had the simplicity of a child combined with the wisdom of old Father William. No mortal could compare with him for ingenuity and inventiveness. He could do wonderful things with a piece of knotted string. There was one thing he lacked and that was a sense of humour; perhaps this was not a loss, for strangely enough it made him all the more humorous.

It seemed wrong, however, to laugh at one so earnest, so guileless and free from cynicism, but at times he was irresistible. Fortunately he was far too busy to care whether I laughed or not. My Good Genius in many ways, he introduced me to new friends and revived old friendships that were almost forgotten. He tempted me along a path which ran quite independently of that followed by my more serious work. He first came to life as Uncle Lubin."*

Uncle Lubin, Heath's first book, is a wonderful medley of the possible and impossible, just as things must look through the eyes of a child. Very few artists can write, and this included Heath when it was a matter of " serious writing." But pure fantasy such as *Uncle Lubin* he could write with ease.

The story is very simple. Uncle Lubin has the misfortune to have his small nephew, Peter, snatched away by the wicked Bag-Bird, a sinister edition of one of the pelicans in St. James's Park. Distracted with grief, he builds an airship in which he flies to the New Moon. At this point the lettering is set in such a way as to suggest the Moon's thinness and slipperiness—an idea which delighted Heath's readers.

The Bag-Bird sees him coming and flies away screeching with Peter, and poor Uncle Lubin jumps off the Moon, but using his coat-tails and hat as a parachute he lands quite safely on the Earth. He then builds a strange boat and after various adventures he finds the Bag-Bird on top of an iceberg. He thaws it with a candle, and down falls the iceberg on to his head, and again the Bag-Bird flies away.

Next he builds a submarine, and after an alarming encounter with a sea-serpent which he destroys by putting salt on its tail, he lands and meets with a Dragon-snake which terrifies him.

* Ibid

UNCLE LUBIN'S DREAM

FROM *THE ADVENTURES OF UNCLE LUBIN*, BY W. HEATH ROBINSON
—*Courtesy of Chatto and Windus*

However, "After a little while Uncle Lubin's courage returned. He remembered to have heard that when you meet a snake or for that matter a Dragon-snake, the best thing to do is to charm it with music. Fortunately Uncle Lubin had with him his old concertina. On this he at once began to play some beautiful tunes.

" The Dragon-snake was quite pleased with Uncle Lubin's playing and began to dance to it. Indeed, the snake danced and danced all night through, and by morning it had danced itself into such a tangle and tied itself into so many knots that it died."

The pictures exactly suit the story. There is a brilliant decorative effect in the black and white drawings of Uncle Lubin's dream in which he sees a host of fairies, goblins and butterflies; and in the illustration of his adventure with the unfortunate Rajah whose nose was being bitten by a wasp which nobody could persuade to go away, there is a delightful touch of absurdity. Uncle Lubin settled the matter heroically by shooting the insect with a blunderbuss !

The book, which of course ends happily with the discomfiture of the Bag-Bird and the joyful reunion of uncle and nephew, was not a best-seller, but a great many children loved it and even wrote to him about it. One little boy asked leave to call his hedgehog " Heath Robinson " as a tribute to the author, and H. G. Wells remarked in one of his books that children regard *Uncle Lubin* as a rare good thing; and he wrote to Heath from Little Easton Rectory telling him that he was " adored in this house."

Uncle Lubin gave great delight, but it did not bring Heath very much money. Knowing that he would soon be wanting to marry, his Good Genius cast round for a more lucrative line of work and hit upon the idea of drawings for advertisements. Nothing could have been further from the artist's thoughts than this kind of work, and knowing little about business, he was suspicious when he received a letter from Mr. Charles Ed. Potter, of Toronto, the London representative of the Lamson Paragon Supply Company. Mr. Potter explained that he had read *Uncle Lubin* in a bookshop and that the author was just the man to illustrate some advertisements which he was writing; would he come and meet him at Tranter's Hotel?

Heath had recently been involved in some unfortunate Law Court proceedings in which he had unsuccessfully sued the creditors of a bankrupt publisher for whom he had done some drawings, so he was on his guard against Mr. Potter and demanded payment in gold. Mr. Potter looked at him benignly through his goldrimmed spectacles and made no objection at all. A deal was arranged, his whimsicality was given free play, and the extravagant fantasies which flowed from his pen sounded a new note in advertising.

Heath Robinson's friendship with Mr. Potter, and later with Mr. J. M. Evans, a director of the firm, lasted all his life. A great many letters passed between them, many in a bantering vein.

For example, in January, 1926, Mr. Evans wrote: " I suppose you know that your reputation amongst engineers is very high, although I have recollection of telling you once that the damned thing wouldn't work, but you shut me up with your reply that that was the humour of it. Apparently, however, some of your engineering feats on paper are studied with considerable interest by the engineering profession, and if perchance you find some valuable invention coming out, copied from one of your drawings, you may be able to prove " anticipation " and get a slice of the patent royalties. This brings me to the point as to whether you did not anticipate the Tank. I would not mind seeing you down for a £50,000 award and being able to prove your case with the published date of one of your plans and specifications."

To this Heath replied: " It is very encouraging to have confirmed once more the interest which my engineering feats have for engineers, and I hope that your belief in them will be strengthened likewise. I always felt that you were just a little sceptical about the practicability of my designs and that it was this nervousness, may I call it, which prevented you commissioning me to reorganize the machinery at the Lamson Paragon Works. It is not too late now, but perhaps we had better leave this matter until we meet again."

Mr. Evans says that Heath was usually a very quick worker, but that he was extremely conscientious and became so completely immersed in his work that he could hardly come down to earth afterwards. He would twist his legs round the table legs when working, and even his face into a resemblance of the model which he had in mind. Faced with a knotty problem, he would sometimes take days, or even weeks to work it out to his satisfaction. He could draw anything, except a well-dressed man or woman. Once, when drawing a Lamson Paragon advertisement, a brother artist helped him by putting in the boots, which he made as down at heel as he knew how, to suit the wearer. But Heath was not at all satisfied and asked him why he had drawn " Bond Street models."

His work for Lamson Paragon lasted for many years, and Charles Robinson also drew for the firm. A list of Heath's drawings numbers about 200. After a while other firms began to see the possibilities of this new kind of advertising and he was kept busy on this sort of work for most of his life.

Gradually his humorous advertising work developed and joined hands, so to speak, with his caricatures of the Machine. A good example is the work which he did for Connolly Brothers, the curriers, whose Leather College on the banks of the Wandle inspired him to some extraordinary bovine fantasies.

Heath shows the New Cow shaking hands on arrival with the headmaster, who presently gives him a caning

CURIOUS PLANT IN AN OLD MEAT WORKS, FOR CONVERTING OLD
MUTTON INTO SPRING LAMB TO MEET THE SEASON'S DEMANDS
—*Rough sketch* (*unpublished*)

to ingrain a correct surface. Rising from his dormitory
bed next morning, the cow, standing on an insulated
board supported on upturned wineglasses, is given
electric drill to eliminate warble fly, and his hide is

H.R.—D*

dried by very dry lessons in geometry. After courses of eurythmics to loosen up his skin, and sunbathing to give it a delicate tan, he is slimmed on a diet of lemon and vinegar, if his hide is needed for baby cars, or cushioned with button mushrooms if his ultimate purpose is an upholstered armchair. Should he be required for morocco leather, he is fed on dates by fat gentlemen in turbans, or if for a perambulator hood, he is exercised wheelbarrow fashion by a uniformed nursemaid.

Heath also wrote and illustrated a little essay on what would happen in a leatherless world. He showed City gentlemen carrying their office correspondence in tin kettles and saucepans, fathers of families stropping their razors on cats' tails, huntsmen mounted on eiderdowns in place of saddles and leading hounds on pieces of knotted string, footballers playing a "sissy" game with a bundle of rags for a ball and knotted clouts in place of boots. Best of all, an hysterical lady motorist with an umbrella shooing away clouds of clothes moths from her cloth-upholstered car.

The preposterous fancies inspired by Uncle Lubin had been simmering in his mind for some time. At first he did not take them seriously and used them merely to amuse children. But he was surprised to find that many children took them in deadly earnest, whereas grown-up friends thought them extremely funny. Even so, he found it hard to believe that the general public would be amused by anything so naïve, especially as the current ideas of humour were so different.

Editors of humorous journals were more circumscribed in their notions of humour than they are today. *Punch* amused its aristocratic readers with jokes about social gaffes, technicalities of hunting, shooting and fishing, with a great deal of explanatory matter to assist the understanding. *Ally Sloper's Half Holiday* specialized in comic inebriation and chronic financial embarrassment. *Judy's* ideas of humour sometimes expressed themselves in a weekly blot competition. *Pick Me Up,* after weathering an attack from prurient critics, tried courageously to introduce a new note in humour and perished from lack of readers. What hope was there for an artist whose humour fell into a new and unknown class?

Heath collected some of the best of his humorous drawings, screwed up his courage and called on an art editor. He was kept waiting for a long time while his drawings were sent upstairs. At last he was called for and found the editor gravely perusing them. Following an awkward pause, the editor said that they were very interesting, but pointed out that he could only accept work which made his readers laugh. Heath replied that this was precisely what they were intended to do. This seemed to astonish the editor who inquired if he ever did what he would call "serious work," and on hearing that he did, remarked: " Well, if this work is humorous, your serious work must be very serious indeed."

However, there were other editors who saw humour in them and were willing to try them on their readers as an experiment. One of these was Clement Shorter, editor of *The Tatler,* who was a little half-hearted and did not employ him for long. More encouraging was Bruce Ingram, editor of *The Sketch*. This journal had been floated off from the *Illustrated London News* in 1893 with the idea of commenting on current affairs in a more lighthearted way than its dignified parent. It started vigorously, with covers designed by Linley Sambourne and with Phil May illustrating the humours of football. Harry Furniss, Louis Wain, Raven Hill, Bernard Partridge, Maurice Greiffenhagen, S. H. Sime, and many others drew for it; but gradually photographs crowded out the drawings until they almost disappeared.

But before this happened *The Sketch* had launched Heath on his career as a humorous artist. *The Bystander* took him up and so did *The Strand Magazine,* which commissioned a series on crime in his burlesque style. This was so popular that *The Sketch* published a series of Heath Robinson skits on blood sports, which included many never before dreamed of, and a little later the famous " Great British Industries " in which his extravagant imagination took wings and soared.

It is probable that Heath hoped that his humorous drawings would meet with moderate success, though even this much is doubtful; but it is certain that the *succès fou* which they achieved took him by surprise. Editors can usually gauge an artist's popularity by their circulations. Tom Browne put up the circulation of a halfpenny comic to 600,000 a week with his Weary Willy and Tired Tim. Just what Heath did for *The Strand* and *The Sketch* is not known, but letters began to trickle into his postbox, many of them enclosing fanciful suggestions. His "British Sports and Pastimes" made such an impression that one of the games, "Bouncing the Beecham," was actually played in India with the costumes and the rules copied from his drawing. His fame spread to other countries.

In America, *Life* awarded him the 250-dollar prize offered for the best illustration of a quotation from Benjamin Franklin, " God helps them who help themselves," and a flying ship exactly copied from a drawing of his was seen in a winter carnival on Saranac Lake. Still more significantly, the term " Heath Robinson contraption " passed into the English language and is frequently heard to this day, even in solemn debates in the House of Commons. No other artist can claim such a distinction as this. Curiously enough, the phrase is now fully fledged and has so to speak flown away from its parent. Young mechanics use the expression without

HOW TO DRAW THE CORK WHEN YOU CAN'T FIND THE CORKSCREW
—*Courtesy of Central Press, Ltd.*

realizing its origin or knowing that a man called Heath Robinson ever existed!

What was there in these drawings of machinery which made even the most hardboiled industrialists laugh? What is it which raises them above the commonplace level of mere knockabout comedy? The Heath Robinson machines are not merely incongruous, they have a special sort of incongruity which is peculiarly appropriate to the Machine Age. As I have tried to show elsewhere, the Machine is always ready to become a tyrant and it is necessary to laugh at tyrants if we value our freedom. Hogarth, Gillray, Rowlandson, Bunbury, Cruikshank, and many others have "debunked" the tyrants of their day, whether individuals or institutions. Now came Heath Robinson to debunk the Machine. He showed that just as a human being can be caricatured or a book parodied by a selective process of exaggeration, so it is possible to caricature machinery by inventing and drawing pieces of apparatus which although "practical" inasmuch as they might really work, are ludicrous in their disparity between purpose and result.

Something has already been said about the complexity of the Machine Age and the growth of Machine worship. Heath struck at this, though it must not be supposed that he had any deep purpose in mind, or indeed any other than drawing something to amuse. His machines are fantastically complicated, and their purposes—as, for instance, putting mites into cheese— absurdly anticlimactic. With monumental ingenuity of invention they achieve results which could far more easily be arrived at by hand.

Time, the other tyrant, is also parodied. The solemn, top-hatted operatives who control the levers and work the windlasses, swinging precariously in mid-air, often stare fixedly at watches. And just as Gillray drew the misplaced surplus flesh and Goya gave men the heads of asses, so Heath Robinson made every piece of his carefully contrived pieces of apparatus imperfect; the wheels are never quite circular, the vent-pipes are in rough sections, and every pulley is made of heterogeneous lengths of knotted string.

It is not obvious at first glance on what fragile foundations the delicate superstructure is built. If the central idea were forced, these conceits would be no more than tedious fabrications; but they are spontaneous, and their joyous spontaneity makes them alive. Although the antic vein of humour hangs upon the magisterial solemnity of his characters, the careful elaboration of detail and the most painstaking meticulousness of grouping, there is nothing laboured about the total effect. Everything depends upon some childlike idea which strikes home with the force of its naïvete. Many artists have tried to imitate him, but all have failed. In Germany, for instance, Paul Klee, who invented a " Twittering Machine " which made birds sing when you turned a handle, missed the essential something. That is the trouble with all his imitators : they do not put any real

AN INTELLIGENT ENDEAVOUR TO RECAPTURE THOSE LONG LOST SPRING FEELINGS IN THE EARLY MONTHS OF THE YEAR

—*Rough sketch (unpublished)*

feeling into their inventions. But Heath was different; he inspired his absurd processes with his own exuberance and made them egregiously plausible.

It was a favourite habit of his with some of his intimate friends to assume the impossible as a truism and defend it with unanswerable arguments. He does the same thing in his drawings. Starting with an idiotic hypothesis he begs the question with the air of a professor of economics stating elementary facts, leads us through a Looking-glass Land of inverted logic and confronts us with the preposterous result so blandly that like Alice we have to think hard to see where the catch comes in.

" First you take an upright stick," said the White Knight, explaining his plan for preventing hair from falling off, " then you make your hair creep up it, like a fruit tree. Now the reason hair falls off is because it hangs *down*—things never fall upwards, you know."

Alice walked on for some minutes puzzling over this idea. Some of Heath Robinson's drawings would have puzzled her in just the same way. The essence of the illusion is the apparently complete conviction of the artist in his apparatus. If there were the least hint of a leg-pull the whole thing would fall to the ground; but there is none at all. On the contrary, he draws as would a mechanically minded infant miraculously endowed with the gift of drawing.

Such humour, like surrealist fantasies, demands very clear and precise drawing. The slightest vagueness of outline would weaken the illusion. So these sketches are extremely definite in detail, with nothing left to the imagination. You can see each bolt and knot, and you can almost count the claws on the strange half-plucked fowls which came to be known in his family as " Heath birds." If you observe these drawings carefully you will notice another thing: each is beautifully balanced in

TESTING ARTIFICIAL TEETH IN A MODERN TOOTH WORKS

A PARTY OF BENEVOLENT PHILANTHROPISTS REWARDING THE
PATIENCE OF UNFORTUNATE FISHERMEN

A NEW METHOD OF CURING FLAT FEET AND RESTORING THE
NATURAL ARCH TO THE PEDAL EXTREMITIES

THE NEW CARD SHUFFLER AND MECHANICAL DEALER FOR BRIDGE
PARTIES

pattern and is satisfying because of the skilful decorative treatment. The work which has been put into it is enormous.

Let us analyse one of them. " Testing Artificial Teeth in a Modern Tooth Works " illustrates a good many of his special characteristics. The congregation of venerable gentlemen who are concerned with the tests have their counterpart in the creaking apparatus somewhat resembling the winding gear of an early coalmine. In ridiculous contrast to this are the dishes of roast pheasant into which the teeth are to be plunged by the ponderous machinery. A shower of fragments at the foot of the machine represents the unsuccessful tests. Three men in shirtsleeves are shown in a subterranean repair shop attending to the teeth with files and mallets, while a senior operative descends with some more teeth laid out carefully on a board, his face an owlish mixture of solemnity and self-importance. A sombre background of brickwork and smoking stacks suggests heavy industrial operations, while the effect is heightened by the gravity and intentness of the entire company, and their complete lack of suspicion that there could be anything absurd in the proceedings.

CHAPTER X

MARRIAGE AND FAIRYLAND

IN earlier times the Robinsons and the Lateys had always been in close touch, and often they would meet at home parties where everyone joined in games of dumb crambo and charades, and sing-songs at the piano. John Latey was a great actor and the children were immensely impressed by his impersonation of Henri Quatre. Sometimes Charles Darling, afterwards Lord Chief Justice Darling, would join in the fun; he was a very clever amateur actor. There was also a persistent business connection between the two families, for John Latey became editor of *The Illustrated London News* and *The Sketch* before the days of Bruce Ingram.

Finally, the bonds were cemented still further by Heath's engagement to Josephine, daughter of John Latey, whom he married in 1903.

Their first home was a furnished flat in the Holloway Road, at the top of a tall building, served by no lifts and next door to the Holloway Empire. Although cheerful, this had its disadvantages. Heath wrote: " Our evenings were enlivened by occasional bursts of applause which we could hear through the wall separating us from the theatre. When we were entertaining and conversing with friends, the applause would sometimes occur at inopportune moments and make an unexpected commentary on our conversation. It was disconcerting, for instance, when in the polite pause following a guest's declining a second helping a burst of clapping intervened."*

Uncle Lubin saw that the financial position was unsatisfactory, and soon slightly bigger cheques from editors allowed them to move into a more comfortable flat in Cathcart Hill, Highgate, which they furnished themselves. Here their two children, Joan and Oliver, were born.

At this time Heath Robinson was working in town in company with Tom, Charles and other artists who occupied studios in New Court, Carey Street. The lower rooms were rented by lawyers, but the artists, nearer heaven, were under the eaves and in the roof, where the rents were only £12 to £20 a year. Business dealings between landlord and tenants were on a peculiar footing. When a new tenant arrived the others would immediately call on him and warn him on no account to pay his rent up to date. It was up to him to be at least a quarter in arrears so as not to let down his impecunious neighbours. The secretary of the estate would also hasten to pay him a call and use shock tactics to induce him to pay on the nail.

The Robinson brothers had separate studios up different staircases. A friend remembers Heath in those days as a young man with steady grey eyes and thick brown hair, reminding him somewhat of the portraits of Fred Walker. His manner was quiet and reserved and he never seemed to get excited. Other artists might throw fits of temperament, tear up their drawings and stamp on the pieces, but this was not his way. He was never in despair, or at any rate he never showed it. There was a very firm will under his mild appearance. He always seemed to know just what he wanted to do, and he set about it with determination. After his father died, suspecting that his death was accelerated by ex-

* My Line of Life.

cessive smoking, he gave up his pipe for twelve years. At the same time he was often extremely absent-minded, perhaps owing to his abstraction while thinking out ideas.

A friend says: " I used to visit him in his studio where he sat with his feet wrapped round the legs of his chair, making his astonishing drawings. He drew and I talked. . . . When teatime came he would perhaps go to the cupboard hoping to find something to eat, emerging with a small piece of rather dusty and decidedly yellow butter, and part of a stale loaf which he hurled into the fire. When the bread was well alight he would retrieve it with a fork, remarking: ' You take toast, I suppose? ' Then with a magnificent gesture of hospitality: ' Draw up and don't spare the viands.' "

" I remember going up to his studio one evening," writes another friend, " to ask him if he was ready to pack up. He assented and began to put his drawing and materials away—that is, put them in a place which he probably wouldn't remember next day—and then he began pacing up and down the room deep in thought, though he was supposed to be preparing to leave. I noticed that he had a great black smudge of ink or charcoal extending from the corner of his eye across his cheek and down his chin. I drew his attention to this. He walked to the mirror, took out his handkerchief and just gave the smudge one very perfunctory rub, not really looking at it at all—and resumed his abstracted pacing, occasionally answering questions I put to him, but in a very absent way. I pointed out to him that he hadn't removed the smudge at all and he went to the mirror again. This time he put a corner of the handkerchief in his mouth to moisten it and gave the smudge another single rub, but without really looking at it properly, and then began to put on his overcoat. I told him he couldn't possibly go out in the street like that because he hadn't removed the smudge at all. He said : ' Oh, damn! ' walked to the mirror once more, gave another rub and said : 'Anyhow, it doesn't matter; anyone can see that it's an accident and that I'm not really dirty.' " Even when they were grown men, a brother artist remembers Heath's mother sending both him and Tom from the table to go and wash their hands!

His clothes and even his manner of dressing were always rather peculiar. Once when he had to go to some public dinner, instead of shaving before dressing, as anyone else would have done, he put on his dress shirt first, with the result that he cut his chin and a large drop of blood fell on the centre of his shirtfront. Finding, to his dismay, that he had no second shirt handy he painted out the blot with chinese white; but the resulting patch of matt-surface in the middle of a highly glazed expanse of white was very obvious.

All through their married life it was an anxious time for his wife when he went out to dinner in evening clothes. Once he succeeded in making himself quite immaculate down to his waist, but when Mrs. Robinson went to his bedroom after he had left, for the very necessary business of tidying up, she was horrified to see his dress trousers still on the bed! He had gone out wearing his blue serge trousers, but on being told about it on his return he was quite unperturbed, or pretended to be. " I don't see that it mattered," he said. " My legs were under the dinner table all the time."

But although not a " dressy " man, and at times absent-minded, especially in the days of his youth, he was reasonably careful about his clothes in the latter part of his life. He seldom had a new suit, but when he did order one he gave a good deal of thought to the choice of cloth and was particular about the cut of it. It would be a mistake to imagine him a slovenly Bohemian.

In the New Court days his studio was as untidy as his dress; he never had any particular place for anything, so he never knew where to look for what he wanted. There was a long table on one side of his studio which was piled high with old sketches, books, rolls of drawing paper, and a mass of miscellaneous rubbish. It was the same a few years later when he worked at home.

" One day he rang me up," says a brother artist, " and asked me if I could help him by supplying him with a reference for a drawing he was at work upon. I think it was some rare animal he wanted. I sent him a small natural history book which just met the case for him. It happened that after a few weeks I myself wanted that book, so I rang him up and asked him if he would send it to me. In a few days' time I rang him again, and he said he had been trying no end to find it and would send it directly he succeeded. After several more applications I gave the matter up, but one day, about a year later, he rang me up and asked if I would come to dinner and spend the evening with him. ' And you remember that natural history book you lent me some time ago,' he said, ' well, it's just come to the top and I advise you to come and collect it before it gets submerged again.' "

He was a frequent borrower of drawing and painting materials, not because he had none himself but because he could never find them when he wanted them. He had the same sort of untidiness about his pockets. Most men keep certain things in certain pockets and always know where to find them. But Heath never did. If he had a cold, or wanted to sneeze, there was always a frenzied fumbling in his pockets for the necessary handkerchief. And when he went into a shop and bought something, the shopman usually had to wait quite a long time while he produced perhaps twopence from a waistcoat pocket, sixpence from a side pocket of his jacket, something from his trouser pocket, or even from a pocket of his overcoat.

He had the most whimsical ideas about money and banking. Once on his way from New Court to get some lunch, he asked a friend to lend him a florin to pay for the meal, promising to repay him immediately after it. As at the time they were walking up Chancery Lane, past his very bank, the friend asked him why he didn't cash a cheque there and then, but Heath replied very seriously that he could not bring himself to draw money out of the bank on an empty stomach!

He was always very kind and generous, especially to young men. A junior clerk in a firm of publishers came several times to his studio to fetch the illustrations he was doing for them. Heath would chat to him, sometimes about books. One day, after the painters and decorators had been in—" Brothers of the Brush," he called them—he needed help to remedy the acutely miserable state of things in which these inconsiderate Brethren had left him. The young clerk gave him a hand and thought no more about it. But a few weeks later he was surprised and delighted to receive from Heath Robinson a bookplate designed specially for himself. This he thought was all the more charming, as Heath was particularly busy at the time.

In 1909 Heath Robinson and his family emigrated to Hatch End, Pinner, which in those days was still open country. As a boy he had explored as far as here on Saturday excursions, but it was Tom, the family Columbus, who rediscovered Pinner with the idea of " taking possession and founding a colony on the banks of the River Pin." Tom, in fact, was already living there, and the inn sign of Queen Anne, which he painted for the " Queen's Head " in Pinner village, swung outside it until the house was altered and became the " Queen Elizabeth."

The two brothers resumed their close friendship just as if they were still boys. There were other friends, too, both old and new. Ernest Huson and his wife, Heath's next-door neighbours, were afterwards almost next-door neighbours when they moved back to North London. There was Thomas Newman, the adventurous bank manager who seemed to know half the interesting inhabitants of London, and Bert Thomas, with his love of the country and his lively sense of humour.

Heath Robinson was now beginning to make a name for himself as an illustrator. In 1908 Hodder and Stoughton published a magnificent edition of *Twelfth Night* illustrated by him in colour, and in 1914 this was followed by a similar edition of *A Midsummer Night's Dream.*

These two plays are rather the ones you would expect him to illustrate. *A Midsummer Night's Dream* is a young man's play, a joyous fantasy expressing the very spirit of rural England and that elfin world which is now half smothered in the smoke of factories. The rustic humour of Pyramis and Thisbe was exactly the sort to appeal to him, and the Wall is a piece of stage property entirely in line with the Heath Robinson tradition. As for *Twelfth Night,* the brainless antics of Sir Andrew and the incongruous buffoonery of the drunken Sir Toby must have tickled him as much as the egotistical folly of Malvolio.

Less to his taste, one would think, was his commission to illustrate *Rabelais,* which was published in 1913. This was fantasy of another kind, a coarse, exuberant clowning which hits hard at the baseness of human nature. Heath let himself go and scored a distinct hit. More than ten years had passed since Phil May had said that he greatly admired Heath Robinson's gifts of " serious illustration," and in those years he had increased his skill and elaborated his technique.

—*Rabelais (Navarre Society)*

These powers found expression in a new and more ambitious book for children written by himself. Probably the idea came to him with the fairy stories which he told his own children when they were in bed.

One of these began: "Once upon a time there was a boy called Henry de Trouville, as bright a lad as ever stepped upon the banks of the River Loire. He had a little brother called Guignon.

"One day Henry said to his father: 'Father, may I go into the forest and gather mushrooms?' 'Certainly, my boy.' 'May I go, too?' asked little Guignon.' 'Certainly not!' 'Do let him come, father,' said Henry. 'Well, go and ask your mother,' said his father.

"So little Guignon went to his mother and said: 'Mother, may I go with Henry to gather mushrooms in the forest?' 'Go and ask your father,' said his mother."

Then there was the tale of Percy Drift, who, disobeying his parents, wandered about and got lost, but after alarming experiences was found again under dramatic circumstances. Also the story of Willy Scrimmage, and Bertie Frimple, whose pathetic poverty was relieved at the last moment by the good offices of a little green elf who popped out of a large green egg.

The charm of these bedtime stories lay as much in Heath's expressive manner of narration as in the quaintness of the plot. Sometimes he related imaginary dreams which invariably ended with his falling down and a voice saying: "Get up, Will!"—and his waking up to find Mrs. Robinson by his bed with a cup of tea.

These stories were never illustrated or written down,

—*Rabelais (Navarre Society)*

but they contained the germs of some of the ideas which came to flower in *Bill the Minder*. This remarkable book, with its wonderful illustrations, shows one side of Heath's character more clearly than anything that he ever did.

Bill was a young man who cleaned the boots, and nobody suspected him of possessing a genius for minding children; but actually he had read all the books ever written on the subject, discussed it with the most knowing professors, and he was even well known in the Minding Room of the Patent Museum at South Kensington. The result was, he became so notable as a Minder that he aroused intense jealousy among his rivals, some of whom became so cross and fractious that they had to be minded themselves.

Now follows an inspired description of the great annual Minding Tournament held by the Duke to celebrate his birthday.

" Everybody was there; the Duke and his Duchess with a handsome bouquet of marigolds and groundsel presented by the wives of the policemen; the Duchess's cousin, the chatty old Viscount, and his sweet young wife; the stout old Marquis who (as every lady knows) is also Admiral of the Regent's Canal, and his six old-maid daughters, who all arrived in bath chairs. The General was there, as a matter of course, with all his medals beautifully polished, and his pockets full of Pontefract cakes and peardrops to throw to the children. At least twelve Bishops were present, besides the Vicar and his eight Kind Curates, who made themselves extremely pleasant to everyone.

" All the mothers and fathers of the neighbourhood were present and minders were continually arriving to compete for the prizes. There were at least one hundred policemen to keep order, and the music was provided by the band of the militia, lent for this occasion by the kindhearted General. Each member of the band performed on a separate harmonium borrowed from the Vicar. Refreshments also could be had by everyone who could prove that he or she was hungry."

There is a true Heath Robinson touch about the tournament tests. In the first, a well-pinched baby and a glass of milk were placed at the end of the course, and each competitor had to run to them balancing a new-laid egg on a spoon, and on reaching them beat up the egg in the glass of milk and pacify the child with this beverage in the shortest possible time.

Bill won it, and a roar of harmoniums also announced his victory in the second contest, in which the competitors had to run carrying three babies, surmount obstacles, place the babies in three empty prams, wheel them back, and discharge them into the arms of the Duke, all without a single cry of protest.

On winning the third event, for minding seventeen tooth-cutters and three indigesters, and sending them all to sleep in three hours, forty-five minutes, he was presented by the Duke with a gold-mounted feeding bottle. The rage of his rivals was now almost beyond control.

" But far worse was to happen when Bill presently carried off the Great Cup for remaining shut up in a bathing machine with twelve vaccinated children for twelve hours. Then they quite lost their tempers, and Bill very nearly lost his life. At least seven babies were hurled at him, as well as the cup and the bathing machine, and Bill was only saved by the seven mothers of the seven hurled babies who rushed forward to grapple with the hurlers, and carried Bill and the babies out of their reach.

" This shocking disturbance caused the Vicar and his eight Kind Curates to faint, while the Duke, who now having lost all interest in the proceedings was only waiting to give away the prizes, turned quite white and at once drove off with the Duchess in his motor, and never again referred to the subject. The General stripped off his medals in despair and gave them away to the children to cut their teeth with. The chatty old Viscount became dumb with astonishment, and the twelve Bishops, with heads erect and half-closed eyes, walked off to their cathedrals. The harmoniums were all put out of tune and quite spoilt by the efforts of the bandsmen to drown the noise, and the tournament was completely broken up."

Bill then became the Minder *par excellence*, and shepherding a band of children, he set off on a series of adventures. On their travels they fell in with a dethroned monarch, an ancient mariner, a good aunt, a Sicilian charwoman, a lost grocer, and other strange characters. There is something of Carroll and Lear in the description of the tournament, and a good deal of his love of tramping in the development of the story.

This book was published in 1913, and in the same year an exhibition of the illustrations was held in New Bond Street.

Interviewed by the Press on writing and illustrating for children, he was asked whether he found that children have the same sense of humour as grown-up people. He replied: " It is somewhat difficult to say. My experience taken generally is that humour as understood by grown-ups is of later growth, but that to broad humour, such as the humour of a chair being pulled away from someone about to sit down, they are very sensitive. The very smart child, the child who gives a quick answer back, is more inclined to be witty than to be humorous. But children are intensely sensitive to the grotesque, and one must remember this so that one may interest and amuse without frightening them. I don't think children's books ought to be made deliberately childish; and in writing or illustrating children's stories one should remember that children are always trying to live up to you, and they resent your trying to live down to them. Their world, limited at first and gradually growing wider, is a very serious thing to them, and their questions go to prove this. One of the best children's books, I think, that ever was written is *Struwwelpeter*; it appeals to all children because it takes their world seriously."

Bill the Minder (Constable)

THE LORD MAYOR HELD A LONG COUNCIL

CHAPTER XI

THE FROTHFINDERS FEDERATION

HEATH ROBINSON had none of the English-
man's love of ball games or blood sports, but he
found intense satisfaction in country rambles. In Hatch
End he was often joined by his brothers and by friends
from London for long walks in the country. These
were sometimes quite adventurous. Once in summer
the party took the last train to Chorley Wood and
walked by moonlight all night through the woods and
meadows, nearing Denham by sunrise.

A faithful walking companion was P. B. Hickling,
and another was S. Jacobs who had been an artist friend
of Heath's when his studio was in New Court. Jacobs
was reputed to have a reliable bump of locality, whereas
Heath, as he himself admitted, was apt to lead the party
astray. In London it was said to be an alarming experience to go about with him. Often he was so deeply
engrossed in some Heath Robinson idea that he had no
notion where he was going and was in constant danger of
being run over.

These rural expeditions became so popular that a
walking club was formed under the convivial name of
" The Frothfinders Federation." Tom, Charles and
Heath were members, and so was their youngest brother,
George, who had gone into business. George was the
biggest of the four brothers; he had an extraordinary
joie de vivre and a fine bass voice. In the first war he
became an amateur assistant blacksmith.

The Perpetual President of the Federation was Philip Pimlott, who according to Heath had been presented by his fairy godmother at his christening with three gifts. He was to become a talented etcher, an accomplished stepdancer, and one of the best boon companions a man could wish to meet.

Other artists, writers and men of wit joined the Federation, and the walks would usually end up at the Crown Inn, Stanmore, or some other friendly hostelry, where they would have a dinner and a sing-song.

"There must be something pagan in me," Heath Robinson wrote, " for whom these choruses had an almost religious sublimity. I do not think there is anything which so closely unites a group of people as a chorus. Especially is this so when it is inspired by good ale, beef, vegetables and friendship. For a few minutes you are completely at one with each other."*

Gradually an elaborate ceremonial was built up round the Federation. Amusing menu cards were drawn and painted by the artist members for some of the dinners, ludicrous poems were composed, and Charles Robinson drew up a magniloquent Frothfinders' Charter.

I WILL ARISE AND GO
TO MY FROTHFINDERS

THE RETURN OF THE PRODIGAL
WATERWORTH OCT· 8 1910 A·D·

* *My Line of Life.*

One of the menu cards which has come down to us has an engraving on the flyleaf showing a precocious infant sitting like a mediæval alchemist among skulls, learned books and retorts. This is supposed to represent "The Illustrious Third Chairman of the Federation, Charles Robinson Esquire, depicted in the Supreme Moment of the Conception of the Idea of Acquiescing in its (the Federation's) Institution, at the Age of Eleven Months."

Then follows an explanation that Charles Robinson is son of the fifth Baron Pembleton of Townley, and that he traces his descent through Hannibal, via Tamerlane and Barbarossa to Charlemagne; then touching by a side issue Boadicea, he reaches the present family by the pre-emption of Lobengula by Nell Gwynne. He married Grizelde Ellalinu Pilbright McOrduery, daughter of the well-known duchess. They both have issue.

Now comes an epic, written by an ancient bard of the family who wishes to remain anonymous:

EKTÉ BENIZIN CANTICULA

Lord of a thousand Frothfinds
In whose eyes glisten a thousand stars in the ensuing sunrise
lift up thy head

Shout lustily to the mountains
That glow so yellow in your eyes of bile, even when they look blue to everyone else
Keep off the grass

The beasts of the field lower at the thunder of your face and the weight of your feet in the morning,
Catch hold of the sky

Sight of the seeing orbs, that see not when they
have finished seeing twice that is once,
Gaze at thine eyes.
Arms that reach o'er a hundred hills, and hands
that cannot clutch at the right lamp-post in the
star time

List to thy gaping.
Feet whose resting place is the great Crown,
The Crown at Stanmore, while thy head wan-
dreth o'er the rooves of the Empyrean,
Cry loud for Marsh or Tommy.

" Ekte!   Ekte!! "
(The ancient war cry of the Pymbilletonnes.)

Finally the menu:

Soupe Clair à la Tommasso

Pain Crumblé   Sal Poudré

Boeuf bouilée à l'homme en chair

Dumplings à la Jacobs   Carrots en Wilhelm
Tournips à la Wyatt   Parsnips à l'Evans
Pommes de terres bouilées au George

Mouton Roti

Spruts à Bruxelles   Toppé du Tournips
Pommes de terres cooké en Archie

Tartalets du Pommes à Dodson

Cheddar à l'Americain   Gorgonzola aux centipedes
Cress du l'eau
Ognons du Printemps
Pain Froidé   Des Couteaux   Des Fourchettes
Serviettes à la Bon Marsh
Condiments au Couronne Stanmore.

When H. B. Waterworth, a member of the Federation, went to Australia, there was a farewell dinner in his honour, and a Frothfinders' Lament was written by Charles, printed for circulation, and chanted by all four brothers.

This was a most imposing composition:

CHARLES: Oh, why begat ye me, oh my parents, that mine eyes should witness this unhappy day? Laugh, oh my spirit, and clench oh my toes in anguish —he is Gone from the White Road, the Dusty Road.

GEORGE: No more does the fieldfare peewit in the Wilderness, nor the Curlew deck his nest with the Curly Black hair of the passing one.

TOM: There is darkness on the Moorland, and the jaded frogs bleat for their absent friend.

WILL: The Cottager's Daughter goes no more astray at eventide, and no man tendereth his Cattle in the byre. Her kerchief blows no more in the night wind, and the duckpond enticeth her not.

ALL: For he is gone from us, and his sword rusts upon his axle-trees, and his Carburettor blurts forth no more in glee upon the White Road, the Dusty Road.

And so on, until Charles solemnly adjures him, "Walk thou in the straight path, not of convention, but of well-doing and uprighteousness withal. Look neither on the right hand nor on the left, shunning the eye of the white-livered woman and the enticements of the Harlot which languisheth," etc., etc. To which Brother Waterworth has to assent.

On his return eleven years later, Heath designed a wonderful card showing the members, grown old and extremely bent, welcoming Mr. Waterworth, wearing wings and holding a harp in one hand, a pot of beer in the other, descending on a cloud which he shared with a kangaroo!

Mr. J. M. Evans, himself a member of the Federation, sent out an invitation to a welcoming dinner at Pagani's Restaurant.

"Bring your cymbals, drums, fifes and fiddles," the invitation ran, "and a good appetite, and don't put on your beautiful dress clothes."

Early in its history the Federation gave an annual tea-party for children, in London, and towards the end of it there were dinners to which ladies were invited.

Suddenly it came to an end. Just why it ended so abruptly is something of a mystery. Looking back on it, the Federation seems very much a part of the world which was shattered by the two World Wars. It belonged to a time when there was gaiety in the air, when beer was reasonably strong, and food rationing was not even a small dark cloud on the horizon.

CHAPTER XII

HEATH ROBINSON PASSES INTO THE DICTIONARY

TO the public nothing is quite so funny as a parody on an institution which is deeply revered, and dignified by ceremonial rites and traditional rules of procedure. The Robinsons, as is clear from the buffoonery of the Frothfinders Federation, were very fond of parody. Heath had already scored heavily with his caricatures of hunting and football, and it was only a matter of time before he skitted horse-racing.

He did this in 1912 in a scene called "Epsom Ups and Downs" which was part of the revue *Kill that Fly*, at the new Alhambra Theatre. His backcloth, which looked like a cross between a racecourse and a switchback railway, and his surrealist starting machine were marvels of imbecile ingenuity. In a published drawing of the last, the familiar top-hatted septuagenarians preside over the starting mechanism, which includes a handbell, a railway signal, a bandsman's drum, a rifle, and a row of boots to give the spindle-shanked steeds a smart send-off. As a further incentive to a quick getaway, a row of mangle-wurzels dangles invitingly before their noses from a long bar in front of the starter.

To add to the piquancy, "Mr. Ascot Heath Robinson" wandered about the stage in check trousers, a fancy waistcoat and an enormous bow-tie. Since Heath was not a professional actor—though sometimes an enthusiastic amateur one—he was impersonated by M. Renée Koval.

This sketch was somewhat submerged under a tide of no less than twelve tableaux. Strikes, eugenics, politics, and the invasion of London by Scottish, Welsh and Lancashire plays were some of the topics, and there was a prophetic scene of Socialist Britain, when the lily-handed inhabitants of Park Lane should be compelled by the wicked Lloyd George to take to shopkeeping. Some of the critics were overpowered and went home to bed before the performance was over, and "Epsom Ups and Downs" got less mention than it deserved.

By this time the phrase "Heath Robinson contraption" had become a dictionary term for an absurd impracticable gadget. It is hard to say when it came into use, but one of the first times the phrase was heard in public was in the House of Commons a few years before the first World War when a Member who had seen an air display in Austria said that the machines were "Heath Robinson contraptions."

Such use of an artist's name was unique. As K. R. G. Browne wrote in the introduction to *Let's Laugh*, a collection of Heath Robinson's humorous drawings published in 1939: "It is not everybody whose name becomes a household word in his own lifetime. Even rarer is the citizen whose name is promoted to the rank of adjective and incorporated in the nation's language. It follows, therefore, that a man who achieves both these distinctions has some pretty exceptional qualities.

"Cases in point are Hansom (and his cab), Wellington (and his boot), Gladstone (and his bag), and Heath Robinson (and his contraptions); and of these cases the last-named is surely the most deserving. Almost anybody, given a little time for reflection, can invent a bag or a boot; even a cab is not really hard to evolve if one is reasonably hackney-minded; but only Heath Robinson could do what Heath Robinson does."

Mr. H. G. Wells wrote to him again. He said that after an illness he had restored his spirits by reading back numbers of *The Sketch,* searching for drawings of his, and that they gave him a peculiar pleasure of the mind like nothing else in the world. He told him that he had discovered a " Heath Robinsonville " in a place called Buntingford, and that sometimes he motored over there to look at certain houses of which Heath might have been the architect.

This was all very pleasant, but Heath Robinson wanted to be a serious illustrator, and his fame as a caricaturist of machinery had become so great that the public, which always likes to label and docket a man, had put him in the pigeonhole: COMIC ARTIST-INVENTOR and could not imagine him as anything else.

This restricted his opportunities. Once when Tom was doing a series of illustrations for the earlier books of the Bible, the man who was responsible for this edition suggested that Heath might illustrate the Book of Revelations with drawings similar to those which he had done for the Poe poems. On meeting Heath he was surprised to find that he seemed "a deeply religious man." Heath told him that he would very much like to do the illustrations, but unfortunately his name had become a byword for a mechanical absurdity. Not long ago, he said, he had wanted to illustrate the life of Christ, but the publishers had been almost shocked at the idea.

The truth is that he felt rather badly about this, but philosophically he laughed at his misfortunes. "I had never been asked to submit rough sketches for decorating the interior of St. Paul's Cathedral," he wrote, " but were I capable of doing so with the most beautiful frescoes, I am afraid that the Dean and Chapter would not have considered the proposal. . . . Even without my signature, there would have been a temptation to imagine in some biblical Patriarch or Prophet a remote resemblance to a figure seen in a different connection elsewhere in my work."*

Another time there was a chance of his getting a commission to decorate a church with pictures of the Stations of the Cross. He would have given anything to do it, but again he was ruled out owing to his fame in the humorous line. Bishops and clergymen were unusually bigoted in this respect. One church dignitary on seeing some of his Poe drawings was so puzzled by the absence of comic machinery that he was completely at a loss, and could only force a hollow laugh at what he supposed was humour too subtle for his comprehension.

Like Edison, he suffered from rumours and Press fabrications. Among the marvellous inventions credited to Edison was a shirt which would last for a whole year without going to the wash. It had 365 very thin layers of a certain fibrous material, and each morning you simply tore one of them off! This intriguing piece of news was published in five hundred papers, and the result was an enormous mail from wash-weary readers all over the world. Letters, some of them with cheques, poured in on the inventor for more than a year, and nothing could kill the story.

All this originated from a visit from an over-enterprising reporter. Several such interviewed Heath Robinson. They would dart hopeful glances about his rooms expecting to find a sort of Mad Hatter's Castle. They asked him if he discovered his ideas in dreams, assumed that he had been trained as an engineer, and as if encouraging a child they assured him that all his inventions would work.

"No doubt," said one of them, "your house is full

* *My Line of Life.*

of your devices, for bringing coal up to the studio, hanging out the washing, and so on. Now tell me about the contraptions which I'm sure you must have fitted up for communicating from one room to another, and all that sort of thing. You know, you must be a useful man to have in the house."

Receiving no encouragement from Heath, he fabricated an article which duly appeared, acquainting the unhappy artist with many things about himself which he had never even imagined.

It was in this way that a disturbing myth was built up —the myth that he was mad! Most probably it originated in the somatic penumbra of a London club. It is easy to imagine some Gentleman of the Old School gravely perusing Heath's plan to catch conger eels by hovering over them in a balloon and luring them to the surface with a concertina.

"The feller who thought of this must be mad," he would snort. Fellow members would agree with him, and soon the story would go round that art editors were employing a harmless lunatic. Those who did consider his drawings amusing would agree, for are not Genius and Madness close allied?

The story grew and became more circumstantial, with copious embroideries. Once this absurd rumour of his insanity nearly lost Heath a commission. His agent, at that time Mr. Ernest Boot, had interviewed the client, an American, and the matter was arranged except for a talk with Heath Robinson. Next day Mr. Boot rang up the client, and to his amazement he was told that the work would have to be cancelled because the artist had been taken away to an asylum overnight! Mr. Boot had some difficulty in reassuring him and making him believe that he had seen and talked to Heath that very morning and had found him in his usual health and spirits.

In writing this biography I have been assured by several well-meaning informants that Heath Robinson spent the last ten years of his life in an asylum; and according to one story, his two brothers came and fetched his drawings from the asylum and finished them before they appeared in print. But the truth is that a saner man never lived. He was so sane that he was able to laugh at the ridiculous story of his alleged insanity and to bear no grudge against those who fathered it.

He was so sane that he saw clearly that many human aims and aspirations were turning back on themselves. One of the first drawings to bring him fame was a skit published in *The Sketch*. This showed a Professor following the tracks of a strange bird whose footprints he could see in the desert sands. The Professor was so completely engrossed in his task that he was quite unaware that the bird was following *him* and peering curiously over his shoulder!

This reversal of hunter and hunted is an almost perfect caricature of the way things turn out in this Age of Science. We invent machines to serve us, but we find ourselves serving them; we build up an elaborate financial system which enslaves us; we release gigantic Forces of Nature which threaten to destroy us. The bird in Heath Robinson's drawing had come round in a circle so that it was now behind the Professor instead of in front of him. In just the same way the things we aim at come round in a circle and strike at us from behind.

The average man who does not realize this considers himself perfectly sane. Heath Robinson who saw it and showed it in his work was rumoured to be a lunatic.

CHAPTER XIII

LONDON'S QUARTIER LATIN

COMPELLED to wear the cap and bells, it was necessary for Heath Robinson to keep in touch with the Springs of Art, and in 1912 he joined the London Sketch Club. This interesting offshoot of the Langham Club was founded on April Fools Day, 1898, and it has kept up the April Fools spirit ever since, as well as a more serious one of inspiration and mutual help. The original founders included Phil May, Tom Browne, John Hassall, Dudley Hardy, Cecil Aldin, Lawson Wood, Claud Shepperson, Frank Reynolds, Harry Rountree and Lee Hankey. Later on it was joined by Edmund Dulac, H. M. Bateman, Bert Thomas, Alfred Leete, W. H. Barribal and many other artists, as well as by well-known laymen such as Conan Doyle and Sir Robert Baden-Powell.

Most of the members were young men, and every Friday evening in winter there would be a two-hour sketching session on a set subject, followed by a quarter of an hour's frank but friendly criticism of the results. After this the members sat down to a supper and a smoking concert.

The club was an oasis of Quartier Latin in Victorian London. On first visiting it as a guest, Reginald Arkell, the well-known writer and editor, was met on his way up the steep, narrow stairs leading to the attic studio in Wells Street by an empty beer barrel which some playful member had rolled down on him. On one side of the main entrance there was a judas-hole in the upper panels, formerly the door of the old condemned cell in Newgate Prison! Above it, by way of contrast, was fixed a tattered glass sign, " Gaiety Stage Door," another genuine relic.

These were the gay and golden days of humorous art. Youthful talent developed comfortably in the universities of Europe and the studios of Paris. In Montmartre, Steinlen was still inspiring the younger men of his generation, and his lithographs turned the hoardings of Paris into a poor man's picture gallery. Caran d'Ache was drawing his stories without words which have since degenerated into the vapid modern comic strip. Louis Morin, with his delicate, sensitive line, Huard, Forin and Leandre—all these were influencing our own leading black and white artists. In the draughty attic of Wells Street a candle was lit which although it sometimes flickered dangerously has never yet been put out.

Inside the studio you led a truly Bohemian life. At supper time you sat on wooden forms at long trestle tables and drank beer out of tall stone mugs. Most of the members and guests came in lounge suits even in the days when formal dress was *de rigueur* elsewhere. Several gentlemen who came in immaculate evening clothes had their boiled shirts covered with drawings like the pages of a sketch book. This was intended as a protest against starchiness, but it gave so much delight that dress shirts at the Sketch Club immediately became more frequent, and one happy guest whose shirt front bore signed drawings by Phil May, Dudley Hardy, Tom Browne, John Hassall, and others, cut out the front of it and had it framed !

The high spirits of the members effervesced in a great many boisterous episodes, some of which have become almost legendary. Once Phil May rose with great ceremony as if to make a speech of national importance, and coughing gravely, adjusted a pair of spectacles on his nose. Coughing again, he placed a pair of pince-nez over his spectacles. Then he beamed at his audience like a benevolent professor about to explain the Quantum Theory and put on a third pair. By this time his fellow members were agog to hear what he would say, and when he opened his mouth to speak you could have heard a pin drop. But he suddenly changed his mind, and fumbling in his pocket produced yet another pair of glasses. This went on until his nose was bridged by no less than eight pairs. Then at last he spoke. " Tut, tut ! " he said gravely, and sat down.

After the Boer War, Dudley Hardy dressed himself up as the king, with a very small, insecure crown, and a sceptre consisting of a soda-water bottle on the end of a stick. Thus royally attired, he presented medals to various members whose names were read out from an old parchment by Starr Wood. Hardy also organized an imposing parady on the famous Souza Band, himself posing as " Bouza " in a tight-fitting scarlet jacket smothered in tin medals back and front. The instruments were made of papier-mâché with reeds in the mouth pieces. Phil May played the double bassoon in a shooting coat and plus fours; Walter Churcher, dressed as a German Jew with a long tangled beard, produced noises through a flute.

There was an elaborate production of *Hamlet,* with Hardy in the title rôle and Churcher as *Ophelia*; and another time Starr Wood, dressed as a diver, performed wonderful submarine feats, fighting with a gigantic lobster. The water was represented by a cleverly arranged screen and liquid spurted from a bottle of soda-water, and the lobster was cut out of cardboard and painted by Hassall.

Some of these incidents belong to earlier days, but the spirit of the club has remained always the same. Not all the members were boisterous; some, although enjoying the fun, took no active part in the revels. Among these was Heath, who if seen at all was always in the background. Once again this was not due to any aloofness. No doubt he would have liked to join in the practical jokes and the impromptu entertainments, but horseplay was not in his nature.

Frank Reynolds says: " He gave me the impression of a very likeable man, a shy and quiet fellow, but none the less one who thoroughly enjoyed the free robustious Bohemian atmosphere which characterizes the club. He looked to me more like a professor than an artist and gave no sign of that ingenious and impish humour which made him famous. I wish I had known him better."

Another fellow member wrote: " He was much too shy to be amongst the rowdies. My memory of him is a very quiet voice, high-pitched; a shy smile always; he seemed to me to be very like a good-natured boy, rather surprised at everything he saw and heard and always pleased about it."

It is rather a notorious fact that artists and other creative workers are inclined to be prejudiced against each other and are often uncharitable when speaking of other men who are competing with them. Heath did not suffer from jealousy and he was incapable of hatred; all the same, there were some remarks which he deeply resented; for example, he never forgave a smart young man who said that his humorous work was " the product of a diseased imagination "; and he had an aversion for people, especially artists, who were loud and boastful. He could not bear self-advertisement, and for himself he went to the other extreme.

A chance acquaintance of his writes: " I was staying at Torquay at an hotel, and as my stay was a long one, newcomers were usually put at my table. The proprietress one day brought a gentleman along and introduced him as Mr. Robinson. We talked for two days about different subjects, including Art, without my knowing he was *Heath* Robinson—and then *he* didn't tell me. I even mentioned *The Midsummer Night's Dream* which he had illustrated. . . . My husband and I liked him so much—he was so humble and kind."

Speaking of the beer-barrel incident, Reginald Arkell says: "Heath Robinson, while no party to this gay adventure in actual practice, was quite capable of evolving a more ingenious removal of the unwanted club member. Such direct action would have seemed crude; his gentle yet fastidious mind would have dreamed up a less painful extraction. Perhaps a trap-doorstep, or a crack-brained escalator running in reverse."

A time did come when the club members found to their surprise that he was not quite so mild and retiring as he seemed. A party of Sketch Club members paid a visit to the Canadian Pacific liner *Empress of Britain,* which was lying in Southampton, partly to look over the ship, but more especially to see Maurice Greiffenhagen's famous painting, "Champlain Bringing his Bride to Quebec," which hung over the main staircase; and also Heath's decorations in the cocktail bar. These last were pictures of crazy apparatus for cocktail-making, such as machines for stoning cherries, polishing them, and ramming in small sticks.

For his own toast Heath stood behind the bar and served the party with what he described as "specials." The toast was given, glasses were raised, and Press cameras clicked. But the next moment there was coughing and spluttering, and Heath laughed. His "specials" were coloured water! The Press photographs looked well enough, but had they been taken a moment later they would have been a dead failure. The victims included such Big Shots as Sir George Maclaren Brown, European general manager of the C.P.R., Lord Herbert

Scott, president of the Federation of British Industries, and Sir Charles Allom, the artist responsible for the magnificent decoration of the ship's lounge.

Although reported in the Press, it is only fair to add that this story strikes his family as so utterly at variance with his character that they do not believe it. Quentin Robinson writes: " It was not his line of humour at all; in fact, he often expressed his distaste of such practical jokes. If there really was coloured water in place of liquor, I suggest that it was somebody else's joke of which he was the unconscious instrument, or that for some reason ' property ' cocktails were used instead of real ones. I can just imagine him *openly* fooling and mixing some crazy concoction for the fun of it, but *not* elaborating a trick such as this."

Gentle verbal leg-pulling of titled dignity was the sort of thing which tickled him, for to the end of his life he could never imagine himself as a Great Man, or even as being on terms of easy familiarity with the big-wigs. " You tell me," he wrote to a friend during the last war, " that you were showing the book I sent you to your friends, and that one of them was a magistrate. Was this merely swank, or do you really know a magistrate? It is difficult to believe. I never knew one, though I once lived next door but three to a J.P."

In the same letter he jokingly described how he had become friendly with a policeman. " Do you remember that one whom we offended at King's Cross many years ago by asking him to lend us sixpence? It is really rather pleasant being friendly with a policeman and able to joke and be familiar with him. Until this levelling war I was always somewhat in awe of them and at least bashful in their presence."

Writing of him in the thirties, Mr. A. E. Johnson, his agent, said: " Heath Robinson has never grown up, and let us hope he never will."

CHAPTER XIV

HEATH ROBINSON, PATERFAMILIAS

FOR *The Child's Arabian Nights,* which he illustrated in rather lurid colours in 1903, Heath
Robinson wrote an introduction which suggested that
he would become a father almost like the sanctimonious
Mr. Fairchild.

" When reading these stories," he wrote, " all children will do well to remember the following. First of
all, they are only for good boys and girls; and if you,
small reader, do not happen to be good, then put the
book down at once and go to bed.

" Secondly, if you have already gone to bed and are
reading these, then you must know that you are not
doing the right thing; so close the book, as well as your
eyes, and go to sleep.

" Thirdly, they are not to be read in bed in the morning, when all should be up and getting ready for
breakfast.

" Fourthly, you must not cry at the stories, nor laugh
too loud; or perhaps the book may be taken from you.

" Fifthly and lastly, you are not to turn up the pictures before reading the stories; or you will be like the
boy who picked out all the plums from the cake and did
not care to eat it afterwards."

Possibly this heavy moral tone was only his fun. At
all events, his children have the most tender memories
of him as a father.

One of the earliest is having boiled eggs for breakfast.

They would hasten to eat them, then turn the empty shells upside down and present them to Heath, who always played his expected rôle. He never betrayed the least suspicion of this sudden, unnatural generosity on their part. Bang, bang would go his spoon through the first empty shell. Amid delighted giggles he would look amazed, incredulous, deeply hurt. Then he would try the next one. Perhaps he would put his ear to the egg as if expecting to hear a chicken cheeping inside it. But no, there was no chicken, no white or yolk. His astonishment and incredulity would deepen, but he would persevere right through the row of empty shells until he came to his own, which was miraculously full, whereupon he would express the most extravagant delight. This pantomime he acted regularly once a week, always to an intensely excited audience, and it was years before his children discovered it *was* a pantomime and not a slice of raw human experience.

At Christmas they had a most wonderful time, as Robinson children always had done down the generations. Breakfast over, they queued up outside the drawing-room, waiting for him to unlock the door; but somehow he always contrived to lose the key, and while they hunted for it all over the house their excitement became almost unbearable. Then at the psychological moment it would be discovered in one of their father's pockets; the door was unlocked and they trooped in. And there in all the mystery of partial concealment were their presents, each lot in a pair of long black stockings pinned to the furniture and garnished with a couple of crackers.

Brought up on Dickens, Heath had all the zest for Christmas of the goblins who tormented Gabriel Grubb. When in later days his daughter, Joan, was a ward sister in hospital, she had only to write to him and say she wanted to make her ward into a zoo for Christmas, and in a marvellously short time the postman would deliver a big cardboard package. In it would be a whole menagerie drawn by her father in bright colours: great red lions, blue elephants, black bears, spotted cows, and perhaps Noah with all his family. If on the other hand she wrote to say she wanted to do " Safety First," he would send her cut-outs of comic policemen and fat suburban ladies crossing roads, pushing prams filled with moon-faced infants. Nothing delighted the patients more. At Christmas everyone came to look at the Heath Robinson Ward, and the tonic effects were as great as those promised in remedial advertisements.

A little later, when the family had moved to Cranleigh, he would take his children for exciting walks down the country lanes. Soon after breakfast they would set out, perhaps down a winding path towards Baynard's Castle, about which he told them gruesome tales of heads in caskets. Other times they walked into the village, trotting along, each in turn carrying a parcel of his drawings under the left arm and his walking stick gripped in the right. Heath would raise his hat politely to everyone he met, as one did in Cranleigh in those days, and he would pass a running commentary as they went along.

" Now Joan," he would say, " you see that haystack over there. What colour is it? "

She would think for a moment and reply " brown," " yellow," or any colour but the right one.

" No, it isn't, it's blue, with grey shadows. The reflection of the sky makes it blue."

Joan would look again, and sure enough it *was* blue, just as he had said. When they got home he would paint the haystack for her to prove his words.

Always he tried to encourage his children's creative faculties. He helped them to build a model theatre, and he invented a series of adventures centering round a romantic cave. This cave existed only on paper, but everything which happened in it, or near by, was drawn by himself, and by his sons Oliver and Alan.

He was pleased and proud of their work, and he encouraged them to come into his studio and be advised, helped and criticized quite severely. Whenever they wished they could borrow his pencils, mapping pens or paint brushes, which stood in a big stone jar by his side. He would even squeeze out great blobs of his best Winsor and Newton paints for the children to use. He also taught them to model in plasticine, make funny faces from queer-shaped stones, draw quaint caricatures on their Easter eggs which their mother had dyed; and when they were a little older, to cut out human figures, trees, animals, and other exciting objects and assemble them to make attractive compositions.

There was one thing he never would allow them to do—copy other people's drawings. When very young, Joan found this rather disconcerting. She and her friends made their own Christmas cards, and her own efforts looked awful to her when compared with cards neatly copied from the slick designs of professional artists.

Heath Robinson was always sketching from life himself. He drew anyone, anything, just as he saw it in unselfconscious ease. He never used professional models, but the mere sight of anything was often enough to make him want to set it on paper. At the seaside he sketched people in deck-chairs, children playing on the sands, boats, gulls, dogs. At home a favourite model was his big ginger and white tom cat, " Saturday Morning," so called because he had been born on a Saturday morning. He always said that this cat knew when he was being drawn by his marvellous poses.

People would sometimes ask the children: " How does your father think of his ideas? " This was a question they could never answer with any certainty. They saw that the business of invention entailed a good deal of pacing up and down his studio. This habit grew so much that whenever Heath was talking he walked to and fro. Later, his two elder sons developed the same habit and it was quite usual to see all three of them chatting in a confined space and pacing up and down, sometimes moving together, sometimes in opposite directions without realizing they were doing it. It seemed to be an integral part of their mental processes.

But evidently Heath Robinson hatched a good many of his ideas *in situ*. A friend succeeded in enticing him away from home one evening—a difficult thing in the case of such a homeloving man—to a dinner at the Savage Club. On the way back, crossing Clapham Common late at night, they nearly collided with a lorry, and in pulling up suddenly the brake stuck. The friend spent the next quarter of an hour on his back under the car disconnecting the brake shackle. Emerging, he found that one of his lifts, a well-known short-story writer, had never even woken up, whereas Heath was finishing a rough sketch for a Heath Robinson brakeless car!

Visitors would also ask: " Is your father funny at home? " and, like the reporters, they would be quite disappointed to see no wheels and pulleys in the drawing-room, or pieces of knotted string slanting from the ceiling. Heath Robinson was certainly funny on occasions, but in a quiet, solemn way which completely baffled people who did not know him. He would enter the room and sit down unobtrusively, and it would be some time before anyone realized that he was wearing a queer garment—perhaps a woman's hat, or a lampshade on his head. Those who knew him well would laugh, but strangers wishing to be polite would glance nervously at the family to see how they were taking it, not realizing that it was just his fun and not some alarming symptom of eccentricity. With a perfectly straight face he would sometimes carry on an apparently serious conversation, the absurdity of which would suddenly strike you. For instance, he would explain with feeling that he always ate porridge sandwiches for breakfast and that " Ratchet " was his favourite girl's name. Among the humourless this conduct may have sounded an uneasy note of suspicion; on the other hand there were people who could not bring themselves to believe that he could be serious at any time, and who imagined that nearly everything he said contained a hidden joke.

Although he had a good tenor voice he was shy of using it for solos, and even in his own home he could not always be persuaded to sing. When he did, it was likely to be " To Anthea," " Bid Me to Live, and I will Live thy Protestant to be," " The Boatman," " Over the Sea to Skye," " Sally in our Alley," or " The Poacher." His favourite chorus was " The Farmer's Boy," and in this song the whole family joined with delight.

He had a great many friends, both children and adults. Parties of nephews and nieces came to stay, and they all loved Uncle Will. So did children from across the way, those he met on the beach, and bold young autograph hunters who knocked at his door. He never disappointed them. Scores of books bear his signature, and many of them have a quick sketch on the flyleaf— one of his Heath birds, or a policeman, or a polite old gentleman taking off his hat to a lamp-post. Children would write to him from Australia or Canada and send him presents of tea and candies.

In his own home he never played the part of a strict disciplinarian. Once a visitor was shocked to find him allowing his children to go on playing with coal, though they were already black from head to foot. But this was deliberate; he never allowed them to " get away with things."

One day, owing to some small offence, the children were forbidden by their next-door neighbour to come into his garden and play, as they had been accustomed to. They were furious, and in revenge they put bricks on his croquet lawn and punctured his bicycle. Heath was very much upset when the crime was reported to him. He did not beat them but he made them feel very much ashamed, and they never did such a thing again. Their only remembrance of corporal punishment is when their mother beat two of the boys with a thick strip of cardboard from her husband's studio!

Heath was a model father because he subordinated himself and his work to his children and spent nearly all the money he earned, which was considerable, on good schools, lovely holidays, parties, treats, and attractive homes for the family. If any of his children were ill he was all concern for the invalid. He would go out and buy black-currant lozenges to ease their sore throats, wine gums, and his own favourite sweet, raspberry nougat, for their convalescence. For himself he bought scarcely anything except his newspapers and a little Capstan Medium Navy Cut for his pipe.

He seemed to have very little use for luxuries. A friend once gave him a Ronson pipe lighter, and a little later he was astonished to see Heath lighting it with a match. He would never " dress up." Even on his holidays he wore no special clothes, but on the hottest day he would sit in his deck-chair on the beach in his usual lounge suit, stiff collar and trilby hat, with his walking stick beside him, just as if he had been magically transported there straight from his morning walk in Cranleigh.

He believed in children enjoying themselves, and when his own children grew up he left them perfectly free to take up whatever profession they fancied. Years later he told a friend that he considered the lot of parents much harder than in previous generations. There had always been great differences in outlook between parents and children, he said, but in the past these had been natural and evolutionary, whereas now they had become revolutionary. His grouse against the younger generation was that they ignored the past and the ancient faiths. He was a firm believer in human nature and thought that nearly everyone was worth while.

"Each one of us," he said, "is given a bag of treasures, and it is up to us to make the best of it. If we don't we have only ourselves to blame."

CHAPTER XV

LAUGHTER IN THE TEMPLE OF MARS

THE war of 1914 did not come upon us without shrill warnings from an alert minority. In the 1910s headmasters of public schools were preaching minatory sermons from the chapel pulpit, while amateur spies who had been in Germany came down to warn the rising generation of what lay ahead. Most schoolboys would listen half incredulously, and then forget the imminence of national obliteration in the excitement of a school match. The public was rather the same. Somebody once published a preview of how the outbreak of war would be announced in the Press. Across the page were heavy headlines announcing the progress of the Test Match, while in very small letters at the bottom were the words: " Germans Land on East Coast."

Curiously enough, the Germans, instead of trying to lull us to sleep with a false conviction of security, helped our prescient lecturers and preachers by starting a minor war of nerves. Disconcerting rumours of German armed might spread abroad, and a crude series of postcards was put in circulation wherein fearful Teutonic engines of destruction rained death upon us. Seeing some of these, Heath Robinson was quick to seize his opportunity, and shortly before the outbreak of war a series of his drawings appeared under the title *Am Tag*, showing the Kaiser's army making use of the Heath Robinson technique to invade Great Britain. This had a peculiar result.

Towards the end of the war he had a letter from a signaller in a military hospital enclosing a page from a German magazine which he had found in a veterinary hospital near Harbonnières. On one side of it was an article written by some German professor. On the other was one of the *Am Tag* pictures, showing German soldiers in pickelhaubes, perched like sinister birds in the tops of trees, fluttering through the air with wings and tail-feathers attached, stalking through the long grass disguised as stags, dangling apples, grapes and bananas to simulate fruit trees—all spying on a diminutive Boy Scout in the Highgate Woods. Underneath, in German, were the words: " The Germans Come! (German Spies in English Woods). " There is no doubt that all this was published not as a joke but as encouraging evidence of British alarm and despondency.

When war came, the output of the handsome illustrated editions of books which had enjoyed an Indian summer since the beginning of the century quickly shrank, and even comedy took only one direction. Humorous artists had to militarize their ideas. Due to his *Am Tag* series, Heath Robinson had a flying start. Drawings of his depicting German Frightfulness in action which appeared in *The Sketch, The Bystander,* and *The Illustrated London News* were so popular that they continued until the end of the war.

In the early days, none of our artists had been to the Front, and their drawings of the Kaiser's army were based on the Franco-German War. For Heath this was no disadvantage at all. His antiquated Prussians in belted blue uniforms, striped trousers and pickelhaubes were the precise counterpart of the senile operatives who presided over his antique machinery.

His " Breaches of the Hague Convention " showed such dastardly acts as Prussians bombarding the British Front Line with bellows and lung-power to give our tommies stiff necks, driving 'flu germs with sticks and drums into the Allied trenches, and sending over a formation of boiling kettles suspended from kites to scald a British division protected by umbrellas. Some of his ideas were curiously prophetic. For instance, both the onion-whittling by night and the syphons of laughing gas to soften up the British before an attack, foreshadowed the use of chlorine and phosgene; and the two German officers thinly disguised as a farmer and his wife, pulling a gun embellished with horns and two pairs of trousers to resemble a cow, suggested some of the later developments in camouflage.

As a columnist wrote after the war: " I am inclined to wonder why it is that no greater use was made of Heath Robinson's genius by the chiefs of the R.A.F. or the Inventions Board. I know nobody whose ideas are so extraordinarily original as his, and nobody who can develop them with a greater regard for simplicity and for economy of material. If Mr. Heath Robinson had been a German, there is no knowing what might have happened before the Armistice was signed."

Still under the spell of " Gentlemen's Wars "—who could forget Wellington's severe reproof at Waterloo of the gunner officer who wished to fire on Napoleon and his Staff whom he had spotted through his field glasses? —we were shocked and amazed at the German methods of all-in fighting, forgetting that in more than forty wars of aggression they had behaved always in the same spirit. With one eye on neutral America, the German propaganda machine was set in motion to prove that Teutonic Kultur was much misunderstood and the German soldier greatly maligned. This gave Heath another opportunity. In a preface to *The Saintly Hun,* he explained that he was setting forth the fruits of his observations after a series of visits extending over the years to that " gentle and amiable soul, Herr Krupp of

Essen, and that lovable but most whimsical of Sovereigns, William of Potsdam."

This little book, published by Duckworth, contains a series of half-tone drawings, and better still, some striking silhouettes in which the kindly behaviour of the Germany Army, the Kaiser and the Crown Prince carries the German propaganda just over the borderline of sanity. The faces of the patients standing behind the Crown Prince who is benevolently opening a new criminal lunatic asylum in Berlin express the summit of imbecile gratitude, and so do those of the Lower Orders for whom the Kaiser is graciously laying the foundation stone of a new prison. There is a surrealist, garden city touch in the picture of the German troopers helping the young birds to build their nests; and a pretty air about the German officers disguised as Kind Curates instilling lightness of heart into the civilian population after a doubtful victory at sea.

An engine of war which lent itself especially to humorous drawing was the Zeppelin. Heath seems to have been very much tickled by a circumstantial account in the *Bourse Gazette* of a flight in one of these machines which nearly cost the German Emperor his life.

The airship had been most elaborately fitted up for the royal flight to Poland, with working, sleeping and reception rooms, and an observation cabin with a huge magnifying glass let into the floor. The Zeppelin made the flight and landed without a hitch in Warsaw, where the Kaiser was met by the Archduke and a guard of honour. But on the way back things began to go wrong. The engines stopped, and scared mechanics scuttled along the corridors and climbed up the ladders outside. In spite of all they could do the airship began to list heavily and a parachute was prepared for the Imperial descent. The commander telegraphed to earth and the whole countryside was aroused, cavalry and cars flying in all directions.

Everything weighty was thrown overboard, including even the officers' swords; but the Zeppelin continued to fall, until by a great stroke of luck its anchor caught in some trees and it reached the ground without disaster. Besides official recognition by various orders and medals, every officer and man received special rewards from the Kaiser in person.

Heath showed the British public how the German bombing personnel received intensive training in Count Zeppelin's evening clases, and he designed and drew a " Subzeppmarinelin " composed of a barnacled submarine of the Jules Verne period which fired shells upwards and was connected by a crazy iron stairway to a prehistoric airship from the cage of which villainous Germans tipped primitive bombs out of a sack. The objective of this complicated attack was an old lady in a rowboat filled with vegetables!

For these war drawings of his he was lucky to need no human models. Other war artists were hard put to it and usually had to pose as their own models with the aid of a mirror. Mr. Fortunio Matania nearly lost his life in this way. Working late one night dressed as a German soldier, he heard a terrible noise and down came a flaming Zeppelin not very far from his studio. He rushed out of doors and ran towards the blaze. From every direction people were running, mad with excitement and that peculiar lust for revenge which grips those who have suffered impotently in moments like these. As he neared the blaze somebody in the crowd noticed him, and next moment he had turned back and was racing for his life. He had forgotten that he was wearing the uniform of the German Army!

Heath Robinson continued to draw at home. He was commissioned to illustrate several books in his decorative style which must have been a relief from the never-ending demands for his war caricatures. One of these was Walter de la Mare's *Peacock Pie* (Constable) where his gentle, whimsical humour expressed itself in his drawings of the talking fish in the frying pan, old Tillie Turveycombe who swallowed some thistledown and floated away over the meadows, Hans the miller with his three black cats, Nicolas Nye the aged donkey, and Mrs. Macqueen of the Lollie Shop.

As to *The Water Babies,* published by the same firm in 1915, this is one of the best set of illustrations Heath Robinson ever did. His coloured plates express almost magically that faery land which Kingsley contrasted so tellingly with Tom's sordid life under Mr. Grimes, and his silhouettes of the great sunfish, the very distinguished lobster, and other strange marine creatures are full of fishy life and comedy. The " Professor," who was made up principally of fishbones and parchment, who never drank anything but water; who ran backwards and whose pockets were full of collecting boxes, bottles, microscopes, telescopes, barometers, ordnance maps, scalpels, forceps, photographic apparatus, etc., is a real Heath Robinson character.

Towards the end of the war an American syndicate asked Heath to make a series of drawings of the American Expeditionary Force in France. The American Army invited him to join them at the Front, and after the customary red tape and procrastination he reached Paris, from where he visited the port of St. Nazaire, carrying a sheaf of forms, permits, visas, etc., written in English and French. He had never been out of England before, and accosted by an officious gendarme while sketching he became nervous and was slow in producing the correct papers. He narrowly escaped arrest.

Soon after this he returned to Paris, and on the American Army's invitation he went to their battlefront

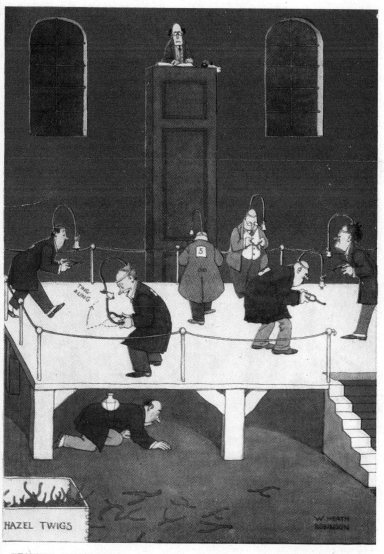

TESTING CANDIDATES FOR THE POSITION OF WATER DIVINER ON
THE METROPOLITAN WATER BOARD

in Old Lorraine. Here he met many American writers and artists; also Louis Raemakers, the famous Belgian cartoonist. One day he was with Raemakers in a dirty, derelict barn, and by way of conversation he pointed out that the dust on the door looked rather like a military scene. Raemakers went over to it, gave it a few sweeps and touches with his hand, and Heath found himself looking at a picture of a cavalry charge!

Raemakers is said to have done more than any other artist to win the war—if anyone can be said to have won it. He was a caricaturist in the Daumier tradition who attacked ideas rather than men, and who plucked the beams from the eyes of mankind in general. All the horror and hypocrisy of aggressive warfare was exposed by his pencil. But there were other artists in a different category who had another function: artists who showed us that even war has its ludicrous side and that a man can laugh at himself and his misfortunes even when he hears Death's wingèd chariot hurrying near. One of these was Bruce Bairnsfather; another was Heath Robinson.

Caricature is both the key which unlocks the emergency exit of laughter, and, in Meredith's words, " the specific for the poison of delusion which folly brings." There was caricature in Gothic gargoyles, in ancient drawings of the gods in Hindu temples, in Roman busts, and in Greek vases. In mediæval times caricature played a great part in baronial courts and even in the churches on All Fools Day. *Hudibras* is a caricature of English puritanism, and *Don Quixote* is one of sixteenth-century blimpery. Caricature is a corrective to despotism, as well as a bulldozer for obstructive tradition and an antacid to miseries too bitter to be borne without the sweetness of laughter.

During the first World War, millions of men found themselves under a harsh and merciless system of military discipline, living lives of almost unendurable discomfort which seemed likely to last for ever. Worse still, they had to face powers of destruction altogether more terrible than any which had faced soldiers before. Warfare had entered a new and more frightening stage. Sergoff and his brother romanticists had given way to robot armies equipped with the deadliest weapons that science could invent. The soldier was forced into a rôle subsidiary to his Frankenstein monster. Bigger and better guns, trench mortars, armed aircraft, hand grenades, minenwerfers, mining and counter-mining, U-boats, tanks and poison gas were changing war into apocalyptic nightmare. The Machine God was in an ugly mood and was demanding blood sacrifice. Hiram Maxim's gun, which the explorer, Stanley, had said would be " invaluable for subduing the heathen," had spawned a horrid brood which threatened to exterminate the Christians.

Heath Robinson's Blow-Bomb apparatus for blowing out the fuzes of Zeppelin bombs, and similar conceits, introduced an All Fools Day feeling into the Temple of Mars, and from the immense correspondence which came to him from men in the Fighting Forces there is no doubt that he eased the tension for those who had to kill or be killed. He was deluged with letters of appreciation, requests for contributions to military magazines, designs for regimental Christmas cards, autographs, drawings for private collections, pictures to hang in messes and gunrooms, and even for emblems to brighten up the guns of batteries! Though his letters of reply are missing, it is clear from the enthusiastic letters of thanks that he hardly ever disappointed his correspondents.

Here is a captain writing from the headquarters of a division asking for a Christmas card, and on receiving a promise of one, proposing a money payment, or failing

this, " Shall we make you a collection of Bosch relics? "
When the card is printed and delivered, he writes:
" Your card was tremendously appreciated by us all, and
instead of 30,000, we wanted about 50,000 copies. . . .
Of course I will get you some souvenirs, and it's no
trouble." He encloses one of the cards signed by the
whole of the Brigade Staff. The picture shows a German
officer disguised as Santa Claus placing bombs in the
Tommies' stockings, which are hung out in No Man's
Land; also nails and tintacks to injure the bare feet of
our men which are seen sticking out from the bottoms
of their camp beds. From a battleship comes a letter:
" We can't thank you nearly enough for the simply
priceless picture which arrived last night. We are all
frightfully bucked with it, especially with the Hun
sitting on top of the Zepp. It's very pleasing to have a
permanent laugh-producer in wartime and it does us
no end of good. . . . I hope next time we're in a civilized
port you'll find an opportunity to come on board. We
shall be awfully pleased to see you at any time of the day
or night, and there'll always be a cocktail ready for you."

The editor of the magazine of a Manchester regiment,
after thanking him for a drawing, writes: " I am afraid,
Mr. Robinson, if we publish the next number of *The
Sphinx* without one of your drawings, the editorial office
will be raided, and not by Zepps, either."

A war-weary officer in the Military Permit Office in
London writes his thanks for two drawings and adds:
" I have one on the office table here, and it cheers me up
when I have *dull clients;* the other one, of the chicken,
makes things merry and bright for the two people who
look after the index file."

A sub-lieutenant in the Navy asks for a drawing to
hang in the mess and adds: " One has only to look at one
of your drawings to envy you the happy existence you
must live in to be able to draw such pricelessly funny

sketches. You don't know what dull moments we have, but . . . we will come and gaze at the picture and realize what the Navy might have been."

Another, after describing the roars of laughter which greeted one of Heath's pictures when it was hung up in the gunroom, says: " Having, I suppose, a certain kink for mechanical details, we fully appreciate the hours of study and labour you must have spent over *The Aeroplane* and such other papers for the unquestionable details of the mechanism."

A man in hospital writes of a book which Heath has sent him: " I have shown it to sisters, nurses and patients and have watched their keenness and delight at the illustrations. It has caused several badly wounded patients to forget their pain."

In the first World War, Heath Robinson became an international figure. Referring to some sketches, silhouettes and books which Heath has sent in for a National Allied Bazaar in America during the war, the organizer says: " Your silhouettes, every one of which was promptly sold, added substantially to the amount we were able to take, and also added greatly to the joy of all the purchasers. My wife and I laughed until we were weak, and we bought three of the sketches for ourselves so that we should always have something to cheer us in dark days. Incidentally, they introduced your work to a great many people. We sold all of your books that we could procure, and a bookseller told us that he had dozens of orders as a direct result of the bazaar. Your pictures make the Germans ridiculous as no others do, and that is very important."

" Do you know," writes a soldier in France, " that it is a bit of history you illustrate now, and that these books of yours are going to last for ever and are intimately associated with this horrible war? "

CHAPTER XVI

MANY INVENTIONS

SO intrigued was the fighting man with Heath Robinson's war caricatures that he wanted to take a hand in the game himself. Scores of letters came in from all Fronts and from every branch of the Forces with suggestions for humorous drawings. Some of these ideas were from majors and even colonels. " I could not help picturing to myself some senior officer secretly thinking of something very humorous," Heath wrote, " and then, disguising the fact of his preoccupation with anything so trivial, surreptitiously posting it off to me."* Many others explained the difficulties in which fighting men found themselves, and appealed to him to invent a way out of them.

" All officers when on duty in the trenches," wrote an infantry captain, " invariably do their utmost to avoid meeting the C.O., as this generally means a long and fruitless walk round the trenches, or else detailing innumerable working parties and also being blamed for anything which in his opinion is ' out of order.' All sorts of schemes are arranged by which the C.O.'s approach is made known to the officer on duty, so that he can take refuge in a dugout, dodge round a traverse or down a communication trench, or conceal himself in a drainage sump, or possibly within a gabian.

" Some of the methods of warning employed are bursts of machine gun fire, telephone calls, scouts and

* *My Line of Life.*

runners, explosive rockets, etc.; by night we fire Verey lights. We have not yet been reduced to the extremity of jumping over the parados into the service trench, but by night we occasionally have to make excursions into the wire, as often as not playing hide and seek to avoid the aforesaid C.O."

He then asks if Heath can improve on these methods. To these letters he invariably replied, often giving his solution either verbally or in a sketch, but unhappily he kept no copies. However, there is occasionally a clue. An Irish officers' mess, weary of returning salutes, who wondered if a machine could be invented to do the job automatically, seems, judging from their letter of thanks, to have received a design for a Saluting Machine consisting of pulleys and pieces of wire.

" It is a matter of deep regret to all thinking soldiers that so many of your excellent and highly practical inventions have been rejected by the Inventions Board," writes a colonel of gunners. " That Board evidently fails to realize that the war is a mechanical one and therefore all mechanical appliances must be good, although some perhaps may be better than others."

After mentioning that mud is found in excess in Flanders, he continues: " Horses have to be exercised, and the result of the exercise is that time and much manual effort are required to remove the mud from their coats. Frequently there is more mud than horse.

" A combined exercising and grooming machine on the lines of the enclosed sketch has been found invaluable. The machinery can be adapted for chaff-cutting and for drawing water, thus rendering the horse almost entirely self-supporting. Hoping that you will give the matter your earnest attention and that the fruit of your labours will not be rejected by the Inventions Board. . . ."

The drawing shows a treadmill made of duckboards

which drives a series of cogged wooden wheels connected by belts of knotted string to a rotary hairdresser's brush.

A major proposes: " A Bee School of Instruction somewhere behind the British Lines in France. Hives of bees are trained under competent instructors to attack and sting to death the wily Hun. Trained hives of these insects are issued to battalions in the fighting line. Before an attack each platoon has its beehive ready, but with the opening shut. On the command ' Bees away! ' hives are opened and the angry bees at once fly over No Man's Land and get to business. The Huns, after being well and truly stung and rendered incapable and incoherent, are then attacked by our infantry. As the Huns are very quick at getting hold of new ideas, it would be advisable in order to distinguish the British bee to have a small Union Jack on each, of course placed in such a position as not to interfere with its business end."

Other correspondents are more concerned with killing insects than with breeding them. From an officer in the Indian Expeditionary Force comes a letter about the Mesopotamian fly. " This fly is not an ordinary fly and we strongly suspect it was made in Germany, so great are its exploits of frightfulness. It scorns flypapers, flytraps, etc., and attacks the long-suffering British officers in overwhelming numbers." Can Mr. Robinson come to the rescue with a suggestion?

Others again want him to exercise his ingenuity in removing insect vermin and killing rats. " We appeal to you as one who has made a close study of animal life and the snaring of all manner of game," says one, writing to him about lice. An infantry officer gives him his own idea of how rats might be exterminated: Dogs, specially trained to eat cheese, could be posted to companies and sent out on patrol. The rats, scenting the cheese inside the dogs, would come out of their holes and so would be caught.

From the Home Front comes a suggestion that moles should be trained to act as guides in districts affected by the lighting regulations.

A captain in the A.S.C. outlines a dangerous enemy plan which apart from the absurd details is curiously prophetic. Speaking of the German minenwerfer which throws a 200-pound bomb, he suggests : " They have provided a number of corks to fit these mortars having a parachute attached to a stick in the centre. On the next occasion when the wind is favourable, a Hun will take his position on each allotted cork and will be projected over our lines. As he descends, he will open the parachute and come down behind us . . . could you, sir, advise us how to combat this nefarious design? "

A signals officer writing from France mentions the great difficulties of maintaining communications between the Front Line and headquarters. " I have, however, invented a way of overcoming this difficulty," he writes, " but before bringing it to the notice of the Inventions Board I should like a drawing showing the procedure so that it may be clear to the meanest understanding. . . .

" The idea is simple. You dig a hole in the Front Line in which you bury some worms. At the proposed headquarters station you dig another hole in which you place a mole to which is attached a telephone wire. The mole smells the worms, digs towards them carrying the telephone wire with him, and this connects by a buried cable the two stations.

" The moles should be hungry before being used, and should be specially trained by the General Staff to dig quickly and noiselessly. They will be taught to dig on a compass bearing or by the stars, in case the Huns try to prevent their work by sending over gas-shells which would interfere with their sense of smell.

" P.S. I am not quite sure whether moles eat worms,

but if they do not, such food as they do like will be placed in the hole to which they have to dig."

An agriculturally minded major of the B.E.F. proposes " A new Terrible Machine—a tank with an enormous Self Binder attached, which mows down the Bosches, ties them up and throws them out in bundles of ten."

Another officer encloses a rough sketch of a new method to flood the Prussian trenches. " A windlass, rope and bucket on one's own trenches is set working, and a row of men pass bucketsful of water from one's own flooded trenches, the last man pouring the water into the Prussian Lines."

" It is considered," he continues ingenuously, " that the Prusians will be so horrified by the attempt that they will not interrupt the service. But in order to safeguard the fatigue party passing the buckets, a row of sentries should be placed on either side of the line of fatigues."

He adds that the flow could be increased by a supplementary service of empty jam tins, Prussian helmets, biscuit tins and shell cases. He also sends detailed proposals for passing flood water from the River Lys to some seaport, by similar methods, and shipping it to Egypt where it could be poured on to the desert.

A few of these ideas which were sent to him Heath Robinson actually used. For instance, sucking the enemy out of his dugouts by vacuum cleaners appeared as the American Suction Tank, and a description sent to him of a soldier laboriously extracting the barbs from barbed wire, one by one, resulted in his famous Barb Mortar.

His inventions in the aircraft section caused so much enthusiasm that a kite balloon section in France wrote suggesting that he should come and spend a week or two with them and give them some ideas of how to haul down a balloon in a high wind.

Many highly ingenious proposals were sent in for dealing with Zeppelin attacks. " What about the following idea," says a young pilot. " Aeroplanes flying over the Zeppelin, one dropping iron filings and another dropping secotine, while beneath are anti-aircraft guns mounted on magnets. . . . Another idea : seven captive balloons each with a bright light under the basket arranged in the shape of the stars representing the Plough, with an aerial minefield arranged between them to catch unsuspecting Zepps who are travelling by means of the stars."

Another writer suggests catching Gothas and Zepps with flypapers and flytraps, while a third has the sensational notion of dropping treacle bombs on the propellers of the Zeppelins so as to clog their working and capture the crews intact. A truly surrealist idea submitted is to shell them with banana skins so as to cause side-slips, and hardly less ingenious is the proposal of a flying officer to employ the R.F.C. to squirt the atmosphere with oil so as to smooth the passage of Allied shells! A lieutenant in an auxiliary petrol company is intrigued with the notion of sending over spies to attach elastic to enemy bombs so that when dropped they will bounce back and blow up the pilots.

Somebody else explains various suggestions which a naval man has put forward for improving cavalry equipment. Among these are an anchor which could be cast in case of a runaway horse, and a windlass attachment on the saddle whereby the horse's head could be wound in when it got out of hand; headlights on the animal's forehead fed by an accumulator attached to a gearwheel which is operated by the raising of the horse's feet; big weights running on rods at each side of the saddle which when the horse reared could be tilted forwards to bring his head down; and props on each side of the animal to prevent him lying down, but on which he could lean for rest when at the halt. Can Mr. Robinson draw these?

Sometimes officers and others ask Heath to help them with the tasks which have been laid upon them by Higher Authority, or they send him quotations from regulations and military instructions which in themselves seem sufficiently absurd for inspiration.

The adjutant of an Australian battalion in France, explaining that an official memo has reached his unit from headquarters demanding that anti-tank experiments be carried out and calling for suggestions, says : " Now, sir, we, the officers of a certain war-worn battalion did our best, but with one accord we decided that you, being so brimful of war and other practical suggestions, are the man to appeal to."

A major in the R.A.M.C. writes to say that a new army biscuit has been issued with a circular memo " Passed to you for necessary action and report as soon as possible," and that several quartermasters have been observed solemnly nibbling at the biscuits to test their qualities of hardness, nutritive quality, and so on. Could Mr. Heath Robinson devise a biscuit-testing machine to save human labour?

A generous brigade major of the B.E.F. writes : " There is a prize offered in this division for the best invention for removing mud from the trenches. So far a number of devices have been produced, rivalling in their ingenuity your engines of war but a great deal inferior in their utility. The prize, I believe, is open to the world, and I thought you might like to submit a sample. I feel sure that you would walk away with the prize if you would care to compete, and I will undertake that your suggestions reach headquarters."

" Why not an engine to facilitate the counting of Austrian prisoners by the Russians? " asks a Canadian lieutenant. " Something in the nature of a telemeter worked by steam according to your excellent designs."

Another correspondent wants a picture of the Austrian Army practising on scooters for the invasion of Italy over the Alps. A flight lieutenant of the R.N.A.S. writes to say that his job of spotting U-boats is made more difficult by jumping porpoises, and he proposes a German School of Porpoises trained to accompany submarines to put enemy aircraft off the scent. An R.E. officer draws an imaginary picture of German prisoners being taken by a huge gramophone playing selections from Wagner, the horn of which is connected to a vacuum cleaner. On Wagnerian lines is the villainous German plan suggested by another writer: the diversion of the Gulf Stream!

Occasionally the suggestions come from civilians. " A lady I know," writes one of these, " heard recently of the formation of a Royal Army Chemical Corps whose duties were to devise some means of combating the gas. She was a university girl . . . and she quite seriously said she supposed the corps would be composed of chemical students who would be posted in the advanced trenches. Being accustomed to smells of all sorts they would have no difficulty, of course, in breathing up all the gas as it advanced. Having thus absorbed it all in their leathery lungs, they would retire, and ordinary Tommies would change over with them." Another civilian correspondent anxious to suggest something helpful, quotes a wounded Tommy as having said to her: " Yes, m'am, the Germans came on like locusts. No sooner had we swept one lot away than others rushed up in thousands. . . . *My opinion is they had incubators behind 'em.*"

A terrible blow at British morale is outlined by a captain of a Manchester regiment: " . . . a series of subterranean passages through England under the golf links. As the New Army officers eagerly watch their putts, a charge of dynamite spurts through the hole. . . ."

A signals officer has a rather similar idea: German tunnellings under the sea to remove British potatoes without disturbing the surface of the ground, the potatoes to be conveyed back along the tunnel in trucks drawn by pulleys and pieces of knotted string.

" I overheard this morning," says an infantry officer, " some fellows discussing the best way for one of their comrades, just off on leave, to test whether a shell he had dug up was still effective. It was suggested that he should suspend his shell over the edge of a wall. He was to take cover on the other side and so arrange it that when he pulled a string his shell dropped on to a brick to see if it exploded. It was a case of either he would know that it was not effective, or his friends would know that it *was*. Immediately I thought of you. . . ."

Here and there a note of humanitarianism creeps into these strange letters. One writer asks Heath to enlarge on the theme that the real reason why the German Fleet is confined to the Kiel Canal is to grow barnacles to feed the German population, and a doctor writes: " I beg to ask that you will kindly turn your attention from methods of slaughter and give the R.A.M.C. some idea whereby inoculations and vaccinations may be carried out with greater rapidity and less effort. My colleagues and I have inoculated about 340 men and vaccinated about 120. One working at a time, it has taken $1\frac{3}{4}$ hours. Surely your inventive genius can lessen the strain? "

This torrent of ingenious proposals continued long after the war had ended. One postwar suggestion was for a Heath Robinson poultry farm in which the tired ex-Serviceman could lie abed and, by means of a complicated arrangement of pulleys, strings and alarum clocks, propel the food for his poultry down a chute from his bedside; and to remedy the effects of the coal shortage another writer put forward a plan in which droves of cats, warmed by small fires, are stroked by the operative staff who arrange for the electricity thus generated to be conducted to the mains.

During the second World War " Heath Robinson " became a still more popular household word. An observation post at the Front was named after him and the Royal Aircraft Factory wrote to say that a jet-testing apparatus had been given his name. " This machine," they wrote, " automatically calibrates jets."

Commenting on this with his usual dry humour, Heath said: " I had never tackled the particular problem of the calibration of petrol jets. I did not realize that petrol jets required treatment of this kind. I had intended giving some time to the study of this, but other matters intervened."

CHAPTER XVII

HEATH ROBINSON AT HOME

SOME months before the end of the war the Robinsons migrated to Cranleigh, which in spite of a
considerable outcrop of suburban villas was still rural.
Heath was struck by the growing attraction of the
countryside for war-weary Britons who had been bred
in cities. In towns, he said, you had to form your ideas
of the country from books, pictures, or even from the
cinema; the weather had not the same significance, and
you were hardly conscious of the changing seasons. This
was at the time when the Pseudo-Antique School of
Architecture was beginning to flourish and old farm-
houses and condemned cottages were being Voronoffed
into retreats for exhausted townsmen. Heath, always
sensitive to constructional causes, said it was hardly fair
to convert a small cottage into a large house by means
of extraneous additions and he settled down in a plain
villa.

He soon found friends in Cranleigh. Lawson Wood,
as gentle as himself in his humorous work and like himself, a little weary of the cap and bells, was living near
by, and one day he ran into a man whom he recognized
as Frank Swinnerton. Then there was Bertram Prance,
the etcher, living only a few miles away at Rudgwick,
and John Eyre, R.I., who, although more than eighty
years of age, would go off into the country carrying his
easel and all his painting materials on his back. Joseph
Longhurst, the landscape painter, was another friend,

but unhappily he died within a few years leaving behind him many unwanted canvases. Heath, as a painstaking craftsman, felt the tragedy of this and wondered what could be done with a dead man's work which it would be sacrilege to destroy, but for which there was no wall space in these modern days of villas and maisonettes.

A shy man himself, it was usually the simple people he liked best. There was a boxer, of all people, with whom he was very friendly; also an old tramp who sold besoms—or rather proffered them half-heartedly, hoping that his customers would pay the purchase price without insisting on delivery of the goods. He became a friend of the family and visited them whenever he came to Cranleigh. Once he appeared with the gift of a miniature besom which he had made specially for Oliver, and another time he came to the door with a gawky youth whom he introduced as his son. " I'm training him in the business," he explained.

Old John the postman who had won a long-service medal was another well-known Cranleigh character. He had a high, squawky voice like a parrot, and he looked like a parrot, too. You would catch sight of him farther down the road, staggering beneath an immense load of mail, but it would be some time before he arrived at your door because he stopped at each house of call for a chat. This was made easier for him because he read all the postcards addressed to each family and he would greet you with the news : " Your Aunt Mary can't come after all," or something of the kind. No one minded his taking a personal interest in their affairs.

Then there was little old Miss Zimmern, who was always dressed in faded black with a small bonnet which might have graced a charlady of the old school. It was only when you got into conversation with her that you discovered what a remarkable old lady she was. A brilliant classical scholar, she had begun to study

SPOTTING FOR SMALL COMMERCIAL PREMISES

STOUT MEMBERS OF THE SIXTH COLUMN DISLODGE AN ENEMY
MACHINE GUN POST ON THE DOME OF ST. PAUL'S

DARING ATTEMPT BY A GANG OF SPIES TO STOP THE RINGING OF
CHURCH BELLS IN WARNING OF INVASION

CONSEQUENCES

HOW THE THOUGHTLESSNESS OF A BUTTERFLY SERIOUSLY
AFFECTED A BISHOP'S CORN

Hebrew when over eighty years of age. Heath on his daily walks would often talk to her. Hearing that his son, Quentin, was studying Latin and Greek at school, she made a point of meeting him and discussing the classics. He was reading Thucydides at the time, and he soon found that she knew Thucydides backwards. She was a relative of Alfred Zimmern whose *Greek Commonwealth* was a great favourite of Heath's.

Heath Robinson took a great interest in his children's education and never begrudged spending nearly all his money on it, but he had pronounced views on how schools should be run. Once the headmaster wrote in his youngest son, Tom's, report: " I am not impressed." Heath exploded. " Damn it," he exclaimed, " I didn't send my son to school to impress the headmaster."

He was very keen on a classical education and more than once said how much he regretted never having been given one himself. He made scathing comments on the way art was treated at Cranleigh School, where at one time it was lumped together with book-keeping and shorthand, all three subjects being taught by the same master.

Tom had been born in 1919, so that he now had four sons and a daughter. All his sons went to Cranleigh School, and to this school went also the son of Alfred Leete and the eldest son of his friend Bert Thomas, who would come over from Pinner with a whole carload of children. Friends of his own children would also visit the house and cousins from Town come to stay so that the house was often overflowing. Heath's peculiar humour puzzled them a little. A favourite joke was to tell them when his birthday was and what he wanted for a present. His ideas for presents were often fantastic, and his birthday dates various and erratic.

In Cranleigh he was called upon by a number of retired military officers who probably came to see him from motives of curiosity. He was not very much impressed by them. In fact, he was very much against the Army as a profession for his sons, saying that Army officers were the most inveterate timewasters he had ever met.

But there was one military neighbour in Cranleigh who won his heart. This was Colonel A., whose big moustache and uproarious sense of fun were a constant joy to a man like Heath. He combined a great fondness for the bottle with a genius for conjuring. In the dusk of a spring evening, Heath Robinson and the colonel came upon rather a sad-looking little night watchman huddled over his brazier near some holes in the road outside the Robinson's house. After trying vainly to cheer him up with boisterous sallies, the colonel suddenly performed a couple of rapid passes and produced a bottle of beer from the watchman's ear! They left him an astonished but a happier man. Unfortunately the colonel's magical gift for producing bottles could not ward off their effects on himself, and not long afterwards he came to an untimely end.

No matter what the weather, Heath always took a daily constitutional by walking to Cranleigh Post Office and back, and according to a friend it was then that he thought out many of his ideas for his humorous drawings. As a relief from this kind of work he did some water-colour painting at home, relying on his imagination, and also some landscape paintings in oils. Sometimes he would go out on expeditions with his friend and fellow artist, Joseph Longhurst, perhaps to the famous White Horse Inn at Shere. This was a true artist's inn; the landlord was himself an artist and Longhurst had painted the inn sign. With Heath, landscape painting was a labour of love, and his Friday evening meetings at the London Sketch Club helped him to keep it alive. He never made any money by it, but he always considered that it played a vital part in his life.

William Latey sometimes came down to Cranleigh and they would walk together deep into the Surrey country. Heath liked treading deserted routes, such as the Pilgrim's Way. His conversation was always interesting. On these expeditions he would speak of the life of the Ancient Britons in the days before they fell under the Roman rule. He had evidently read deeply, and his interests lay with the simple folk of bygone days rather than with contemporary events. One of his favourite authors was Hardy, most of whose books he had read, and a pet aversion was Dean Inge and his ideas on population. He detested eugenics, saying that it destroyed romance and the subtlety of love. Romeo and Juliet were still the perfect lovers, he would say; could anyone imagine Romeo pausing to consider whether Juliet would bear him healthy children?

Always his kindness was one of his most marked characteristics. Unlike many of his fellow countrymen he had no vindictive feelings for the Germans after the war. In Cranleigh he often employed a couple of German prisoners in his garden, and although his hens appeared to lay a smaller number of eggs when they were about, and sometimes only empty shells, he bore his former enemies no grudge. Forbidden to give them food, he would " accidentally " leave two mugs of cocoa and some bread and cheese in the garden shed, and when he returned later he would find that " strangely enough the cocoa and cheese had as accidentally disappeared."

Never did he refuse to do a kindness to one of our own men who had fought in the war. A captain who had lost both his legs in the war wrote to ask him if he could invent some means of overcoming his disability. Heath Robinson sent him a drawing of a legless man encircled by a mediæval belt to which was attached an artificial leg and a series of barman's pulls with which to operate it.

"How will this do?" he wrote. "It is really quite a simple leg, though it would require a rather wide pair of trousers. The levers would work like those I am told are used for beer engines, and you will see that every movement of the leg is allowed for.

"It would of course require some practice to work quickly, but in time I am convinced you would be able to move along quite nicely with it. The lever boards would have to show, they could not very well be hidden in the trousers, but then again they would be useful to put parcels on. . . .

"P.S. I was compelled to put the figure in an under-vest only, but under the circumstances you will realize the necessity."

In another letter he told the captain that he could console himself by drawing a glass of beer at every step if he wished to!

Heath was now almost at the height of his fame, and letters came to him from all parts of the world. The deluge of humorous suggestions showed no sign of abating. One writer proposed a picture "Putting the Springs into Spring Onions"; another suggested "Training Spiders to Cobweb Port Bottles." From South Africa came a description of a severe storm which flooded a hotel dining-room, with the result that the visitors took their meals off the billiard table, sitting on it and passing the salt and condiments with the cues; could Mr. Heath Robinson draw a picture of it?

An author wrote from Dublin with amusing impudence: "I only know you through your delightful cartoons illustrating fairy stories in *The Strand*. Well, listen me own jewel-an'-darlin', I am writing a series of studies of Dublin children for a home paper. Several have appeared, and the circulation of the paper has now

NUDIST NOVICES BEING GRADUALLY ACCUSTOMED TO EXPOSURE
IN THE GROUNDS OF THE NEW NUDIST COLONY

reached 42,000,000 (the non-readers being illiterates
and foreigners). This is very gratifying. Here is a
chance for you to become famous—do a few cartoons for
me—will yeh, oul' burser? (this is a Dublin expression,

means bosom friend). I'll pawn all me clothes an' any little appearance I may have (I'll get a tenner on them anyway) to pay you. I suppose you were once in strait-ened circumstances yourself, so you'll understand my position. People looked aghast at my cheek in writing to you, but I know, even though you refuse me, that you will not think bad of me, for it is only the really great can afford to be kind and gentle."

There is no telling what he replied to this modest appeal, but to another playboy letter from Ireland his answer was as ingenious as his humorous inventions. A naval lieutenant writing from Bantry explained that he found himself in difficulties when out shooting wild duck and pigeon. " We find it extremely difficult to get within a reasonable distance of them," he wrote, " they being so wild and gifted with wonderful hearing. We have tried everything we can think of, i.e. lying flat on our stomachs under camouflaged canvas trying to look as much as possible like a bush, carrying a lump of furze when stalking, using a dinghy while one of us remains on shore. . . . If we can get four pigeon in a fortnight we consider ourselves lucky, and almost the only way of getting them is by discovering a tree in which they like to sit and then lying in wait for them—well, that's hardly good enough, you will admit, it's such an uncomfortable method and the ground is so wet owing to the perpetual rain, and even when we have shot the fourth pigeon, which is necessary for a pie for us two fellows, the first bird has of course been hanging for quite long enough . . . with the consequence that the last bird shot has to be bunged in at once.

" Now, sir, I hope you see exactly our trouble, and could you suggest some device? "

To this Heath replied : " It is rather a curious coin-cidence that some time ago I was one of a small shooting party in the south-west of Ireland and, as in your case, not only was it necessary for us to have pigeon pie but we met with exactly the same difficulties in procuring it. In our case, however, the difficulties were aggravated by our being three in number, and it was consequently necessary to have at least six birds in our pie, and by the time the sixth bird was shot, the first was—well, not worth consideration. Nor, as in your case, could we honestly blame our marksmanship. It does not become me to speak of myself in this respect, but my two friends were excellent shots and often hit their birds, and I do not think that I overstep the bounds of modesty if I tell you that I taught them how to shoot.

" We tried everything—all kinds of camouflage and the most ingenious devices, but could not sufficiently for our purpose overcome the native bashfulness of the Irish bird. At last one of my friends, a well-known diplomatist (whose name it is unnecessary to disclose) threw out the suggestion that the only way out of the difficulty was to inaugurate some sort of central control of the sport, if not to nationalize it, and so to pool all the bags of the district as to ensure an equal and continued distribution of birds in prime condition to everyone.

" I was at this time called away to Siberia to supervise an important engineering enterprise and so was prevented from following the matter up, but I freely give the suggestion to you for what it is worth. If this should not meet the difficulty I am afraid there is nothing for it but Appendrodt's. . . .

" P.S. I think it would hardly be necessary to appoint a Commission to inquire into the matter."

Although writing formal letters came so awkwardly to him that it was said that the house was upset for three days whenever he wrote one, Heath loved composing letters like the above, and it made no difference if his correspondent was a complete stranger.

An American lady observing in an English magazine a nature note about a fish which when it saw a fly rose to the surface and ejected a drop of water which stunned it and rendered it an easy prey, wrote to him suggesting that this was plagiarism and that the fish be compelled to change its name to " Heath Robinsoniensis." He replied : " Many thanks for calling my attention to the infringement of copyright. I have already placed the matter in the hands of my solicitors.

" I cannot hold out the hope to the accused that he can mitigate his offence by changing his name."

In conversation his humour was so quiet that often you had to listen with both ears or you would miss it. He seldom changed his tone of voice in making a joke, but he would make the most outrageous statements in a manner quite matter of fact. One of his " serial " jokes was about a mythological lady named Mrs. McGraskin who was supposed to be concerned with his double life, and by whom he confessed that he had had a large family with fantastic and cacophonous names. When his children were growing up he would speak to them about this lady, who was violently unattractive, with an air of darkest secrecy, and pretend that they were on no account to betray his confidence to Mrs. Heath Robinson. Once he announced with a perfectly straight face : " You know, you are all love children."

These straightfaced jokes completely baffled some people who came to the house : they would hardly know whether to laugh or be shocked. On the other hand there were visitors who had it so firmly in their heads that Heath Robinson was a " funny man " that they would roar with laughter even when he said something quite seriously !

A favourite form of joking with him consisted in reversing the accepted, conventional phrase. A friend who often came down from London to spend the day walking with him was so frequently invited to supper afterwards that at last he felt obliged to say he feared he was eating him out of house and home. The conventional reply would have been: " Not at all—it's a pleasure," but Heath's answer was: " Don't bother about that, old chap. Half a crown in the children's moneybox now and again will make that quite all right."

The same friend remembers playing bridge with the Robinsons and other guests for the modest stakes of a halfpenny a hundred. He had such phenomenal luck that he won more than three shillings. Heath asked him how he had got on, and on hearing of his enormous success turned to the assembled guests and announced that whenever his lucky friend came to the house to play cards he arrived by twopenny bus and went home by taxi.

Except for informal gatherings of this kind, and family reunions, he disliked social functions and was always shy of meeting strangers. He could not bear people who were pretentious, and he hated snobs. Once when some ladies came to the house, it was obvious to his family that their empty talk and affected manners jarred on him, though he tried hard to conceal his feelings. But when they had gone he said: " I dislike women who come to my house and keep their hats on at meals. This isn't a restaurant! "

Another time, after he had visited an eminent author to discuss the illustrations for one of his books, a friend asked him how he had been received.

" Oh, quite all right, I think," said Heath. " Perhaps there was a little feeling of—well, here's the plumber come to see about the job."

His hatred of insincerity sometimes caused him embarrassing moments when amateur artists and art collectors invited his opinion about so-called works of art.

He could hardly bring himself to be critical, but he could not bear easy pretence.

When his real friends came to the house he was a naturally good though unobtrusive host. He entertained more by his spontaneous fun than by taking part in any organized entertainment.

For many years these family gatherings were largely musical evenings. With the Robinsons this once popular form of fun survived long after it had ceased to be fashionable in an age of wireless. Even in later years when the family was dispersed, reunions, especially at Christmas time, were enlivened by homemade entertainment: improvised sketches, a burlesque Russian Ballet in which Heath actually danced himself, and once a fantastic fun-fair with half a dozen sideshows crowded into a small room. Heath contributed drawings for a peep-show which was advertised by lurid and suggestive notices such as " What the Butler Saw "; but the " peeps " were absurdly innocent, consisting of such innocuous objects as Heath Birds!

CHAPTER XVIII

THE HARDSHIPS OF A HUMORIST

SOME artists are unworldly people, full of impracticable imagination, given to fits of temperament,
and with hardly any money sense at all. Heath Robinson
was not one of these. He rejected the idea that artists
were licensed to be muddled thinkers and irresponsible
citizens. Once when he took his son, Quentin, to the
London Sketch Club he remarked to him that it was
good to be in a room full of men who were ordinary
mortals, soberly dressed, most of them good, sound
breadwinners and family men.

He knew very well that his decorative work was his
true *mètier* and the thing that he most wanted to do,
but although commissions to illustrate books still came
his way from time to time, most were from editors of
magazines and from commercial firms who wanted
nothing but his funny drawings. The very word
" funny " began to irritate him; he sometimes said that
he saw nothing funny in his work at all. But he bowed
to circumstance, and helped by Mr. A. E. Johnson, he
continued turning out comic drawings after the war was
over, and indeed, almost to the end of his life.

Mr. Johnson was acting as his agent, but the words
" agent " and " client " hardly describe their friendly
relations. A glance through the enormous file of letters
written by Mr. Johnson to Heath Robinson gives some
idea of the difficulties of a humorous artist's life, and
it throws rather a strange light on British business

methods. Here are a few excerpts for about nine months in the years 1921-22:

" Come up to town with your bag, etc., on Thursday morning ... Ashbee will introduce you to the Managing Director, and they will take you over the works. You are then to lunch with the Managing Director, and discuss the drawings which you are to undertake. . . . If for any reason you fail to catch the train, there is another— but the earlier train should be caught."

" It appears that Ashbee is so impressed by your immense prestige that he is afraid to send you a reminder, though most urgently awaiting the drawing."

" I have just had an urgent call from X saying the roughs you put in for the reduction of price of their toffee, although excellent for future possible use, are not quite what they anticipated. They expected something in your mechanical style."

" I wrote to you about a fortnight ago regarding a coloured label for a tin of household cleaner of the Vim and General Utility kind, for which we had an inquiry."

" Allberry would rather like you to collaborate with Arkell for a four-page Almanack for 1922, to be published in *The Bystander*."

" The man left in charge by the Managing Director appears to be a complete dunderhead, and I have had the greatest difficulty in getting out of him any data for you to base your sketches upon."

" They want you to create two grotesque types, a man and a girl, the former to be called Mr. Smart and the latter Miss Natty. . . . If you badly want to introduce knotted string, the obvious place is the dog's lead. . . . *They must have these drawings first thing Wednesday morning next, which only gives you tomorrow.* . . ."

" Mr. Smart and Miss Natty were well received. We have no instructions to complete them yet, but this is the usual way with advertising work—a fearful hurry and commotion to start with, and then usually a long pause, eventually ending with another tearing hurry, or else the silence of oblivion."

" You may remember sending on a letter from the (Blank) Cinematograph Corporation. These people wanted a sketch from you to advertise " Dandy," a film comedian in whose comedies they are specializing. . . . They think the surrounding sketches should be at least six in number, but naïvely add that if you could make the number fourteen, this would be better still, as there are fourteen films."

" The scheme for a Christmas Greetings Card from X, Ltd., is approved. Needless to say, after all this dilly-dallying they have decided that they want to get the thing out by Christmas. It will be a fearful rush to manage. . . ."

" . . . when they see you they will try to get you to abate your price. You will, of course, refuse to discuss such a proceeding, not merely on principle, but because they have apparently already agreed . . . to pay the figure."

" I have just been asked by the printers if you would introduce the office cat assisting the staff in one of the drawings you have in hand entitled ' Making out State-ments.' Apparently in some offices everybody in the building is called in to assist in making out monthly statements."

" . . . if you could arrange for the tin to be on the end of the rope in some fashion, and slightly tilted up so that the granules may fall down on the gentleman's tongue."

" Also they had great hopes that when you put the cat in, it would be helping in the accounts, and they would feel awfully obliged if you would make the animal sticking down the envelopes. . . . I am afraid they are very fussy people."

" Messrs. Ward Lock have been inquiring very anxiously for news of the end-paper design for their Children's Annual. . . . I wonder if you could let me have one or two more rough pencil sketches to show *Gaiety*. These people have been particularly anxious to get your work for their magazine. . . ."

" A new humorous weekly is projected by Newnes, the editor of which . . . has been exceedingly anxious to get something from you. We told him that it was utterly hopeless to expect any fresh ideas from you for a month or two. . . ."

". . . I fear you must have suffered considerable irritation from the extreme difficulty in giving satisfaction. The trouble is, of course, that your sketches are passed round to the heads of half a dozen different departments. One can never get agreement in that way at the best of times, and moreover, probably each departmental head feels it incumbent on him to make some suggestion or criticism just to show that he is earning his salary."

" They would like the gentleman on top of the ladder pouring sugar from a bag into the tub, and they are also very keen on only one piece of sugar falling on each spoke."

". . . they like the busy appearance of the office, such as . . . the desk, cat, strong-box, and so forth, but they would like the gentleman at the desk to be neat, and writing with an ordinary pen."

" I thought you would probably like to do the nonsense verse for the *Royal Magazine*."

" A rather novel inquiry has arisen. . . . A firm recently started operations which is intending to devise film advertisements to be shown in between the items of the proper programme at cinemas all over the country. The proposal is that one of the film studios should reproduce your drawings as a film, i.e. actors will be dressed up to represent your characters, the necessary properties to represent your various articles of machinery, etc. will be built, and the various episodes of your advertisement reproduced and photographed in motion of course. . . .

" My own feeling is that the scheme attempts to achieve an artistic impossibility. Your ideas and your vein of humour can only be properly expressed through the medium of your own drawings. If one tries to analyse what makes your humour popular, I think the essential thing is that your inventions are sufficiently related to life and actuality to be plausible, once the basic absurdity is accepted, while nevertheless quite remote from it. In other words, your humour is fantastic in the strict sense of the word and your own medium of expression is just the right vehicle for conveying it. If one were to attempt, as these film people propose, to convert your preposterous old gentlemen into real living flesh and blood, and your machinery into concrete facts, it seems to me that the fantasy is broken and the illusion which can be created in one medium is impossible of maintenance in the other. I feel that the actor, however carefully made up, who attempts to impersonate one of your fictitious people would look merely silly, and a model of one of your machines, when shown in actual operation, a merely stupid contrivance. It is the very fact that nobody would dream of putting one of your machines into real operation that constitutes their charm . . . the medium of the film would eliminate just that quality which makes your drawings what they are. . . . My own feeling is that . . . some scenario should be devised whereby your particular vein of fantasy can be adapted to the film's own medium."

" These (Problem Title Picture) competitions have been exceedingly popular, and *The Bystander* proposes to do another in connection with the forthcoming Theatrical Garden Party. They particularly want the drawing to be by you. . . ."

" I am sorry for all the trouble regarding the Theatrical Garden Party drawing. . . . I have a telephone message from *Printer's Pie* that your drawing is now the only thing for which they are waiting before closing for Press."

" The *Evening Standard* would be pleased to have articles and illustrations on any or all of the following subjects: ' Getting Back to Normal Life after Holidays,' ' Mixed Bathing,' ' The Channel Swim,' ' Fishing,' ' Broadcasting.' "

" *Royal Magazine.* Your two sketches approved. . . . *London Magazine.* Four rough sketches approved. . . . *Pearson's Magazine.* I have already written to you about these. . . . that gives you Wednesday, Thursday, Friday, Saturday and Sunday in which to carry out four drawings for *The Strand.* . . . *Nash's Magazine.* We have not yet submitted roughs. . . . *Royal Magazine* wants you to do two pages of sketches as before for another instalment of " Violent Verse for Patient People." . . . It was practically impossible to fend this commission off. . ."

" I am afraid it will be absolutely essential for you to come up to Town for half a day in order to be taken over X's works again. This is most exasperating, as you are so very busy, and it seems to be totally unnecessary. But as you know, many of these firms have an idea that nothing can be satisfactorily accomplished until you have been over the works, and the case is particularly acute with X's because the old man of the firm has got the notion firmly in his head and is clinging to it with the pertinacity of the aged . . . if you do not pay a second visit to the works, the old man in the first place will be convinced that any and every sketch you do is not

TWELFTH NIGHT, Act II, Scene IV. (*Hodder & Stoughton*)

QUEUE DE LUXE

up to the standard of the first book and not nearly so good as it would have been had you toured the works; secondly, he will develop the idea that Mr. Robinson is not giving to the job as much attention as he ought to."

H.R.—G

" They say they are quite prepared not to be believed, but they are perfectly certain from past experience that if they publish the drawing as it stands, certain guileless members of the public will write and ask for a machine of this type. They therefore want you to put a patch over the present machine and draw in its place some quite fantastic article which could not be mistaken either for a true (Blank) Adder, or a cash register of the usual type."

" You will notice that the makers state in their advertisements that one bottle contains 2,400 drops. The idea is that you should do a drawing, in your special vein, of machinery ensuring that no bottle of X is allowed to leave the factory even half a drop short. I think they are expecting to see amongst other details a procession of regretful and tearful old men bearing away rejected bottles which have been proved to contain only 2,399½ drops. Other small suggestions which they make are that there might be on the vats or walls of the factory various dials and meters bearing such announcements as 'Today's output: 137,786,431 drops.'"

Heath Robinson was nearly always invited to go down to the works of the firms for which he drew humorous advertisements, and they found he had a natural grasp of mechanical details. His drawings were firmly based on fact, and he very much disliked drawing something when he had no clear idea of how the real thing looked and worked. In the first World War he was obliged to draw tanks from pure imagination for some months after they had come into use and before a description of them was released by the Censor. But usually he mastered all the necessary details of a thing before he allowed his humorous imagination to distort it. After his daughter had become a nurse, he wanted her to tell him many things about medical matters, hospital equipment, nurses' uniform, and so on. His family remembers him poring over Harrod's Catalogues, and fashion books—somewhat out of date.

Speaking about submitting sketches to editors, he once said : " It's not a bad plan when you have hatched out some ideas that you think are really good, to put in one or two duds for throw-outs." And then he added : " The unfortunate thing is, of course, they choose the duds ! "

Heath was a true caricaturist, not merely a clown with a pencil. The word caricature is derived from the Italian " caricare," which means to overload (a vehicle), or to drag something which is just a little heavier than the means of conveyance can manage. This " overload " comes by exaggerating the most characteristic feature of the subject. Heath drew absurd pieces of machinery, crazy processes bridging the gulf between Means and Ends; and by exaggerating the Means to a fantastic degree, he burlesqued the solemn utilitarianism of the age and struck a blow at Machine Worship.

He visited cement works, tan-yards, structural engineering firms, coalmines, and the factories of firms which manufactured Swiss rolls, toffee, paper, marmalade, beef essence, motor spirit, lager beer, and many other things. Often he would despair of finding any trace of humour in operations which seemed to him so deadly efficient. The operatives were completely absorbed in their work, and he could scarcely believe they would respond to anything so flippant as his irreverent conceits. But he found he was quite wrong about this.

" When their stern preoccupation with the work was lifted," he wrote, " these earnest men were like children out of school. Nothing pleased them more than to see that which held them so tyrannically treated with levity. These were the type of men to which I had to appeal. They were men with great knowledge of machines and whose lives were devoted to them. . . . There must always be this co-operation between the jester and his audience."*

It is remarkable that those who appreciated his caricatures most deeply were the men most deeply in thrall to the Industrial Frankenstein. For them his drawings were more than mere entertainment; they were a means of psychological release. Yet he was able to do more than amuse them; he eased the shackles of a tyranny which would have been unbearably harsh but for a liberating breath of laughter. Dimly the working population was grateful to him. When he went to Glasgow he was interviewed by one of the leading newspapers and, on the day before he left, his photograph was published with an article about himself and his work under the headline: " The Gadget King is Here."

" I had the gratifying feeling," he wrote, " that the whole of Glasgow and Clydebank had been anxiously awaiting my appearance; and now that at long last their craving was appeased they could get on with their work of shipbuilding contentedly."

Engineers and others, heavily identified with technical processes were delighted with his absurdities. On one memorable occasion Heath delivered a lecture to the Sheffield Luncheon Club, which met under the formidable patronage of the Sheffield Chamber of Commerce. His subject was: " The Lost Cord is the Way to Prosperity."

With several pieces of string dangling from his pocket, he explained to the learned members of the club the manifold advantages of knotted string over steel. For Sheffield, he said, string could knit up the ravelled sleeve of care. One of its chief advantages from

* My Line of Life.

a structural point of view was the readiness with which it could be used for joining things, and another was its portability. Whereas no engineer could possibly obtain a portable welding plant, he could easily carry in his pockets a large quantity of string.

" I personally am never without it," he said, emptying his pockets to prove the statement.

Furthermore, string had an adaptability which steel could never hope to equal. If a steel hawser broke, nothing could be done about it, but if a piece of string failed, there was no difficulty about knotting in another piece of string, and with many such knots there was no limit to the ultimate strength of the strand. This was proved by the many knots which figured in his drawings of machinery.

One slight disadvantage of string in the engineering industry was that whereas with string you could pull anything you liked, it had not yet been found feasible to use string for pushing. However, this drawback was not a serious one, because no sane person would want to push when it was a simple matter to walk round to the other end and pull.

He then entertained his audience by illustrating some of his inventions on the blackboard and explaining their purposes. These inventions included his plans for using hydraulic pressure for turning on the shower in the bathroom. He also announced that he had given a great deal of time and thought to the use of coal and its by-products, and that industry would find his ideas very helpful when it had progressed far enough to be able to use them.

He then sounded a cautionary note, explaining that the by-products of coal might swell to such an extent as to threaten the world with over-production. However, he had evolved a scheme whereby the surplus end-products could be returned to their original mineral

state. Already, he said, he had found it possible to de-
compose his toothbrush and reconvert it into a lump of
coal.

His audience was delighted and Heath was presented
with a gold penknife.

CHAPTER XIX

BROADCASTS AND BOILED SHIRTS

D URING the first World War and in the first five
years after it, collections of Heath Robinson's war
caricatures were published and republished by several
firms, but his first " serious " work to appear after the
war was Perrault's *Old Time Stories* (Constable) in
1921.

This was beautiful work. In his coloured drawing of
the princess asleep in the four-poster bed hung with cobwebs, he rivalled his brother Charles in the delicacy of
his line, and his enchanted castles were as mysterious as
Rackham's. These illustrations were even better than
those he did for Elsie Munro's *Topsy-Turvey Tales*
which appeared two years later, although in this last
work there were some striking silhouettes and some
charming coloured pictures, such as that of the cow who
dressed herself in shoes, striped socks, a bonnet and a
green shawl, " went gay " and skipped across a field.

But as the years went by his fame as a creator of
mechanical absurdities grew so great that he was forced
more and more into the commercial line of art; and, in
spite of his retiring disposition, he was persuaded to
appear in public and even to broadcast.

The first time he broadcast was in April, 1923. He
was always nervous when he was called upon to speak
or demonstrate in public, but he was very careful in his
preparations, rehearsing both words and drawings, so
that when the time came he was fairly confident. Al-

though he found the atmosphere of Savoy Hill friendly, he said he thought it might have made things a little easier for him if there had been liquid refreshments on tap.

" But this," he wrote, " I understand has always been against the high principles the B.B.C. have set themselves and so steadfastly maintained."

He was intensely Saxon, and always a little intolerant of intolerance.

In this first broadcast he spoke about his homemade wireless set which he had built from pieces of frayed string, egg cups, a bottle and a kettle, and he invited listeners to make drawings of it from his description and send them in to the B.B.C. There were thousands of entries.

Some time later he again broadcast from Savoy Hill, and with him in the studio was the invaluable Mr. Johnson who had helped him prepare his address. They had agreed on an elaborate code of signals in case he required prompting, but once he was under way Heath did not falter and there was no need to use it.

This time his listeners had been warned to have handy a sheet of paper ruled into numbered squares. With this link between them, he was able to give them a simple drawing lesson, the point of which was that the audience had no idea what object they were drawing until it was completed. The result, if correctly carried out, was a Noah's Ark with a dove perched on top of it.

Apparently even the B.B.C. censorship is not quite puritan proof, for a lady wrote to him saying she was grieved and disappointed that one who held so high a place in her esteem should stoop to making fun of the Bible. Heath was a match for her: he wrote saying he was saddened to feel he had wantonly thrown away the treasure of her good regard, but at the same time he was puzzled to know how he had ever managed to win it!

W HEATH ROBINSON

"ONCE UPON A TIME THERE WAS A NOBLEMAN" (*CINDERELLA*)
—From *Old Time Stories* (Constable)

H.R.—G*

He also promised not to make fun of Noah's Ark again in the same way, which in the circumstances was a fairly safe promise to make.

In 1938 he appeared in the television studio, where he drew and displayed several remarkable devices. One of these was the "Sonata Chair" which enabled a musician to play sonatas while sitting at his ease, and another was a Heath Robinson Car fitted with a television set designed to warn motorists when it was necessary to slow down.

Lastly came his *pièce de résistance,* his Pea-splitting Machine. The announcer told listeners that it was " so vital to our digestion and general well-being that we have persuaded the inventor to bring it to the studio and tell us something of the way in which it is intended to work, and of the mechanical ideas which lie behind its construction."

Heath then came before the camera with his drawing of it and explained some of its intricacies, one of which was a candle. Finally came the climax: the machine was set to work. The inventor daringly applied a match to the candle; there was a terrific report, then silence. Two minute fragments of a pea were displayed triumphantly before the camera to show how efficiently the machine had worked!

Besides a regular demand for humorous drawings from *The Bystander, The Sketch, The Tatler, The Sporting and Dramatic, Nash's Magazine, The Strand, Pearson's Magazine, The Royal Magazine, The London Magazine, London Opinion,* and the *Graphic,* Heath was commissioned by the *Daily News* to run a comic strip, and Uncle Lubin made another appearance, slightly changed, as Mr. Spodnoodle.

Mr. Spodnoodle's popularity was not as great as Uncle Lubin's and he retired early, but his inventors' never weakened, and in 1934 the *Daily Mail,* which was organizing the Ideal Home Exhibition at Olympia conceived the idea of a special Heath Robinson home fitted up with some of his inventions. Heath agreed to this and did the drawings, from which the firm of Venreco, with great skill, built " The Gadgets."

" The Gadgets," which was rather like the witch's house in *Hansel and Gretel*, stood on a site measuring fifty feet by thirty feet, and its irregular roof, with its wild projections, crazy chimney-pots and homemade wireless aerial strung between a pothook and an umbrella, was just under twenty feet high. It was peopled with lifelike figures about two-thirds life size which were worked by electricity. Father, mother, children, cook, general maid, gardener, gardener's boy, cat, cows, were all modelled under Heath's supervision, and the humans were dressed in clothes of his own fashions.

The early morning scene in the house was arranged as a little play in three acts, repeated again and again. On the first rise of the curtain, the master and mistress were discovered in their bedroom, in two single beds, facing one another with their feet resting on a hot water bottle warmed by a candle. The long hand of a clock on the wall was attached to an alarum, which aroused them, and caused a bottle of refreshing liquid to descend on a tray within reach of the old gentleman. Both figures sat up alertly. The curtain then fell.

In the second scene the master of the house was seen singing in his bath, holding on to a length of knotted string which actuated a bucket-showerbath. He sang so lustily that Baynes's band, which was nearby in the exhibition, complained about him. There was also a slight contretemps due to the bath flooding, and finally to Mr. Gadget's papier-mâché feet melting in his bath; but this was not until many thousands of people had seen him at his ablutions.

In the third scene the maid turned an appliance

which looked something like a ship's steering wheel. The end of the spokes beat the breakfast gong, while the windlass wound down the master and mistress now fully dressed and sitting on boards suspended by wires, passing through trapdoors, from the bedroom above. On alighting in her seat, Mrs. Gadget's weight depressed a spring which turned on the radiogram. Her husband by sitting on a concertina arrangement squeezed milk through a tube and so fed the cat. Enormous covers rose into the air, revealing two boiled eggs!

In other parts of the house and in the garden were the Heath Robinson car, the custard-mixing machine which consumed eggs at a prodigious speed, discarding the shells, the perpetual motion automatic laundry, an astonishing Heath Robinson lawnmower, cows which whisked their tails when pecked by a Heath Bird, trees with fanciful Latin names on which grew turnips and carrots, and a surrealist nursery where the cradle was rocked by a clock pendulum and the baby was rotated and powdered by machinery.

This last device, when reported, caused amusement among the Americans who remembered the famous " Automatic Electric Baby Tender " invented by Edison's assistants on the birth of his daughter, Madelyn. Immediately over the baby's head in this ingenious apparatus was a diaphragm like a telephone receiver. If the baby should cry, at the first wail communication was established between this diaphragm and an electric clock, whereupon the cradle was set rocking by a small motor. If the crying continued beyond a certain time, the clock released a lever, and an arm attached to the side of the cradle, operated by a crank carrying a feeding bottle, was swung into the baby's mouth. If hunger was not the trouble, another arm on the opposite side swung over the child's mouth with paregoric, and at the same time the electric current was turned into a set of magnets placed round the cradle, and any pin which might be troubling the child was removed. If the yells continued, the thirty-third Degree was applied. Two arms lying flat in the cradle under the baby were slowly raised and the child was turned over. Then an electric spanker fastened to the footboard spanked it! Edison was delighted with this elaborate joke and said a patent would certainly be granted if it was applied for.

A close friend remembers Heath's agitation on the day when the Exhibition was opened. On this red-letter day his friend remembers him consulting his wife as to what boots he should wear and where all his best clothes were to be found.

On arriving at Olympia he was nervous about whether the elaborate devices in The Gadgets would work when the " Silk Hats " came round. Some of them stuck a little at first but on the whole they worked very well. Rather to his dismay he was lionized. People rushed to see the Great Man, lifting up their children to catch a glimpse of him. And curiously enough they gazed at The Gadgets in embarrassment, fearing to laugh lest it might hurt the inventor's feelings.

Some time after this he was approached by an architect who had designed a fun-fair palace in Blackpool. He was asked to contribute pictures of not very respectable ladies and gentlemen careering round outside the building to suggest the joys within. He turned down this vulgar request. Though far from being a puritan, he was rather fastidious. For instance, he did not mind a rude story if it was really funny, but he detested stories which were merely coarse. Another proposal which he refused was that he should figure as a waxwork in Madame Tussaud's Exhibition. On the other hand he designed a waxwork figure for the Crystal Palace Exhibition in 1934, and in the opinion of some people this was the only live thing in it.

In the same year Hutchinson published *Heath Robinson's Book of Goblins* from Vernaleken's *In the Land of Marvels*, which was illustrated with several coloured drawings and over fifty black and white pictures. This was in rather a different style from his Shakespeare illustrations or his fantasies for *The Water Babies*. There is the same unusual brilliance of imagination, as for instance in his drawing of the jinnee coming out of the casket which the fisherman had discovered, and the same vivid decorative flair, as in his picture of the woodcutter's daughter kneeling and speaking to the dwarf with a coloured patchwork sack, red cap and pointed boots, with a remarkable decorative background of trees and dwarfs against a humped horizon. But the colours are much more posteresque, and the most enchanting of the illustrations are the many small black and white sketches of gnomes, little men with big heads and long beards, and so forth.

Except for one other small book which he illustrated in the last year of his life, this was the last of his "serious" work to be published.

At about this time in his career a series of his drawings began to appear in the *Daily Mail* and continued for many months. Heath Robinson guyed topical subjects. On his holidays a bored dentist filled in his time by excavating sand pillars, a policeman gonged rabbits on Hampstead Heath, and a burglar spent a busman's holiday holding up a bird with a gun and robbing its nest. He extended the dog-racing technique with the ideas of fishing for an electric salmon with a magnetic bait and using an electric bull for matadors; he brightened up football with a mechanical grass-drier, double-toed boots, and a machine for repairing shorts; Christmas festivities were made safer by a pudding-sifter for threepenny bits, a gadget for ejecting stones from French plums, an expanding waistcoat for emergencies, and

THE FIRST THING WHICH TOM SAW WAS THE BLACK CEDARS
—From *The Water Babies* (Constable)

mechanical cracker-pullers; bridge was facilitated by a shuffling bowl, an automatic dealing machine, and a cover for concealing revokers to save them from embarrassment.

In the year 1935 the Great Western Railway celebrated its centenary, and in honour of the event Heath was asked to prepare a booklet giving his idea of one hundred years of the company's progress. Before the contract was signed, the directors wished to meet him, so one morning Heath set forth with Mr. Boot, a member of the A. E. Johnson firm, to meet the railway magnates at lunch. They knew nothing of the artist apart from his work and evidently they expected to be entertained with uproarious conversational absurdities. But in this they were disappointed. Heath was shy and spoke scarcely at all. Poor Mr. Boot had to work hard to keep the conversation going. He said afterwards that it was a very trying experience.

But the centenary booklet was a brilliant success; Heath did eighty drawings in two months and the directors were delighted with them. *Railway Ribaldry*, as it is called, traces the development of railway travel through an era of surrealist ingenuity. Obese workmen in chequer-patched boiler suits construct the first locomotive, apparently from the pickings of a salvage dump, and when completed the engine is tested for speed by an apparatus consisting of a grandfather clock, knotted string and a bandsman's drum. Night duty at one of the first railway signal stations is carried out by a venerable party in a nightshirt perched on a pile-platform, with the aid of a handbell and a candle, which the engine driver peers at through a telescope. There is a most moving picture of a romantic gentleman seated in an open truck pulling a prototype communication cord of knotted string because he wishes to stop and make honourable advances to a lady sitting opposite

(*Hitherto unpublished*)

THE

PARTY

him; and there is a melodramatic one of an absurdly overdressed lady being ushered into the first " Ladies Only " compartment, while a crowd of elderly admirers in top-hats wrestle with the police in an attempt to rush the primitive barricades to get a closer view of her.

An antiquated method of filling the boiler without stopping the engine shows the locomotive passing under a row of suspended buckets, tin-tubs and watercans, which tip their contents through a funnel fixed on top of the boiler; to clean the tunnels there is a strange contraption of rotary brooms carried on the front of the engine, and a charlady with a mop sitting on the back of the tender, apparently for touching up. The absurdity of the methods of changing over from broad to narrow gauge is intensified by a partly derailed locomotive propped up with umbrellas, and a tray with cocoa and a boiled egg being served to one of the workmen. The ticket collectors are trained by an ingenious series of outstretched hands revolving on a circular belt, and a revolving wheel from which umbrellas are suspended at intervals, with the adjuncts of a peephole and a handbell, is used for the identification of lost property. Heath who seemed to have a weakness for cows could not resist introducing a humane cow-catcher which catches up the cow on a padded board, with a cushion for its head to rest upon and a bin of barley stooks within convenient reach. Towards the end of this inspired history, the G.W.R. took to the air, engine and all, thereby obviating the necessity for tunnels. Heath himself was taken on a gala excursion to Bristol, where he met Sir Robert Horne, Mr. J. H. Thomas, the Lord Mayor of Bristol and other celebrities.

At the close of the year he designed a 140-foot canvas of " Life in the Stone Age " as a setting for the Chelsea Arts Ball in the Albert Hall. Just before the ball, a friend went to see him and Heath said somewhat acidly that some silly ass had suggested he should go to the ball as a Greek god. " Well, why don't you go as a Greek god?" his friend asked. "Why not?" Heath retorted. " Why don't you go as a Heath?" suggested his friend. " A *blasted* Heath," put in his son, Quentin.

This was characteristic of the atmosphere of happy banter which prevailed in the Robinson home when his children were growing up. He never posed as a genius and his family never treated him as such. The very idea of anyone wishing to write his biography, I am told, would have struck him as absurd, and indeed, he destroyed the greater part of his correspondence. His attitude towards the younger generation was not always consistent. He was teased affectionately by his children and he took it all in good part; yet suddenly and unexpectedly he would stand on his dignity. " I resent the familiarity of young people," he said once; and another time he astonished his family by saying that he would on no account be called " Pop " and by suggesting that they should call him " Sir."

One of the things about which his family teased him was his book *How to be a Perfect Husband,* which he produced in collaboration with K. R. G. Browne, the grandson of Hablot Browne, or " Phiz," who illustrated Dickens. They were jointly responsible for several books : *How to Live in a Flat, How to be a Perfect Husband, How to Make a Garden Grow,* and *How to be a Motorist.* They planned these books together, then Browne did the writing and Heath the illustrations.

In these humorous books Heath's idea was always to approach the ordinary things of life from a fantastic angle rather than to indulge in sheer imagination which was not grounded in reality. In *How to be a Perfect Husband,* for example, the utilitarian outlook was neatly skitted by applying it to the highly inappropriate business of marriage. The fiancée's æsthetic sensibility is tested by noting her reactions to the Albert Memorial, and something of Heath's aversion to Dean Inge appears in the prescribed methods of surreptitiously taking her blood pressure, sounding her heart at the cinema and weighing her unawares. Tips are given for adapting fatuous wedding presents to other purposes, and there are descriptions of various devices for dealing with the confetti nuisance. A picture of the married state almost as hideous as Chaucer's is painted by pictures of " Morning Darts " and " Duets on the Trombonium." There are awful instructions about marriage in middle age and how to alleviate its boredom.

These books appeared in the nineteen thirties. On the death of K. R. G. Browne, Heath found another collaborator in Cecil Hunt, and in the nineteen forties were published *How to Build a New World, How to Make the Best of Things and How to Run a Communal Home*.

Heath said how much he enjoyed this sort of collaboration in light humour, and he added a note on the restrictions of an artist when he illustrates serious works. " Authors of more serious subjects," he wrote, " naturally have their own ideas as to the illustration of their works. The artist must be subject to the writer. He may not have too free a hand and perhaps trump the author's tricks.

" But occasions sometimes arise when the illustrator's tendency to enlarge on his subject is excusable and even necessary. He may have to make more illustrations than the subject taken literally affords. He may not, as the composer of anthems is at liberty to do, repeat the same phrase over and over again. He may not make more than one illustration to the same passage. He is compelled to take the slightest excuse for an illustration. I knew an artist who boasted that he once illustrated the word ' the.' I never saw the drawing.

" The well-known classics are the safest books to illustrate. There is no fear of the author's interference."*

Illustrating the books of other men, especially the famous, might involve him in unwished for excursions. He was so contented in his home, so ungregarious, that it was very hard to entice him out, except for walks in the country. However, in 1938, he was introduced at a Foyle luncheon as the guest of honour by Mr. Leslie Burgin, the Minister of Transport, who said : " I never go upstairs to the attic without thinking of the admirable services Mr. Heath Robinson has rendered humanity by his devices to force a fly to leave the top of grandfather's head. His contributions to the drawing, humour and mechanics of the future will never be forgotten. What have Leonardo da Vinci's notebooks to teach him?"

Then according to a fellow guest's account, Heath Robinson, a small, lightly built man with earnest eyes and thinning hair, got up and drew his latest invention —a contraption with which a vorticist, cubist or surrealist could blow out his match when he had lit his pipe, though he had a palette in one hand and a paint brush in the other. He explained with a nice mixture of diffidence and bravado the container full of compressed air at the top of the easel, which was actuated by an india-rubber tube the end of which when kicked smartly by the vorticist extinguished the match.

" It is the very fact," Mr. Johnson had written, " that nobody would dream of putting one of your machines into real operation that constitutes their charm." Yet here were drawings of absurd machines which could actually be demonstrated. At the Royal Lancashire Agricultural Show he exhibited drawings of how electricity might be extended in the farm and the home.

* My Line of Life.

One of his contraptions simultaneously rocked the baby
and stirred the stew.   There was a " combine " which
milked the cow, turned the milk into cheese and then
bored holes in it.   If anyone doubted whether these
machines really could be made, they had only to remember The Gadgets at Olympia.

But as a matter of fact people of an engineering turn
of mind had already observed that the Heath Robinson
contraption was quite capable of working.   This was
one of his secrets.   Had his contrivances been less carefully thought out, had there been the least hint of casual-
ness in the artist's conception of them, they would have
lost their force as caricatures and even their power to
amuse.   But on the contrary, they were so meticulously
contrived that they could have served as blueprints for
constructional engineers.   This was all part of the deadly
solemnity which Heath intended to convey, and the
firm structure of logic which he built on impossible
premises.

One of his competitors manufactured spectacles for the baby and carried the cow... There was a "combine" which milked the cow, turned the milk into cheese and then baked holes in it—If anyone doubted whether these machines really could be made, they had only to remember The Laughter of Olympia.

But as a matter of fact people clearly often kept their presence of mind had already observed that the Heath Robinson contraption was quite capable of working. This was one of his secrets. Had his contemporaries been less careful they thought out—had there been the least hint of real logic in the artist's conception of them, they would have lost their force as caricature and even their power to amuse. But on the contrary, they were so meticulously contrived that they could have served as blueprints for extra-rational engineers. This was all part of that friendly solemnity which I felt impelled to convey, and the faint suggestion of electric which both bewitch us and no possible pretence.

CHAPTER XX

THE STOCK EXCHANGE AND THE MONASTERY

HEATH ROBINSON'S autobiography, *My Line of Life,* was published by Blackie in 1938. Most men write self-consciously about their own lives and cannot resist colouring them up, but Heath detested bombast and he tried hard to be honest about himself. A near neighbour in Cranleigh who had written his autobiography in a rather more flamboyant style and who seemed anxious to be thought on terms of easy familiarity with the famous, hinted rather broadly that Heath Robinson was something more than a mere acquaintance. Heath's typical remark on reading the book was: " I never knew I was such a close friend of his before! "

He was so reticent about his success in the world that even his wife was slow to realize that he had become famous, and he was so critical of his work that he sometimes threatened to have a big bonfire. He was still surprised whenever he saw his name in print. *Punch* remarked that " Professor Heath Robinson " was a likely man to perfect an apparatus for sucking through a hole in the wall one's neighbour's garden soil, and Heath was astonished when a friend showed him the cutting.

His name was used more and more as a catch phrase. Somebody in the crowd was heard to describe a Chinese scaffolding in Singapore as a Heath Robinson contraption, and in later years the chairman of the Malayan

Tin Dredging Company referred to the Colonial Office set-up in Malaya as a Heath Robinson topheavy structure which would not in the long run prove either desirable or effective. There was a stormy meeting at the Admiralty about a concrete jetty which had given trouble and for which someone was being roasted. But a reference to the thing being a Heath Robinson contraption at once changed the whole atmosphere. Everyone laughed and the culprit heard no more about it.

One day Heath Robinson met Low, the cartoonist, at the Savage Club, and a few days later a cartoon appeared in the *Evening Standard* showing Heath and Harry Tate as possible new Ministers in a Cabinet reshuffle. Harry was to be Financial Secretary and Heath Junior Lord of the Treasury. Lord Simon, with his legs twisted in embarrassment, was standing on one side of the " Harry Tate Mousetrap " holding a placard: " Public Demand for Straight-cut Rat Poison." The rats, in top-hats, were in the foreground as profiteers.

Heath wrote to Low complaining that he had given Harry Tate a more highly paid post, and Low replied: " I appreciate your note about that cartoon. I gave Harry Tate a higher salary because he has a larger moustache. May I express the pleasure it gives me to find that you are a real person to whom I can express my admiration."

Low, of course, was writing in fun, but all the same he was expressing an idea which many people had—the idea that the man who fathered such eccentric notions could hardly be an ordinary mortal.

" I don't count Heath Robinson as a human being so much as a joy in life," Mr. H. G. Wells wrote to Cecil Hunt, who sent him a copy of the autobiography, " like early crocuses, watching gulls fly, well-behaved cats, or geese, or a windy common.

" First I went through all the pictures and now I am

reading the book. I don't roar with laughter at Heath Robinson so much as savour and enjoy his cold-blooded, deliberate absurdity. There is nothing else like it."

Heath certainly had something in him which was like early crocuses, or geese on a windy common, but he had another side which was alert, matter-of-fact and very much of this world.

One breezy afternoon, tramping over the Downs with a friend, they came upon a well-dressed, rather stout lady lying prone, her arms and legs spread wide and her open sunshade some distance away from her. Both of them stopped short. Had she had a heart attack, and ought they to go to her rescue? They decided that they ought to, and walked towards her; but suddenly Heath Robinson grasped his friend's arm and said: " Come on, she's quite all right." His keen eyes had noticed a book which was lying at the lady's side, open and carefully placed face downwards.

His grasp of mechanical processes was so sure that his rough drawings were very rarely turned down. He came into contact with finance. John B. Gledhill wrote to him inviting him to illustrate a book which he had written jointly with Frank Preston called *Success with Stocks and Shares,* and Heath Robinson met him in the City. On such occasions he always played the part of a wondering child. " I can't regard you as a real stock-broker without your umbrella and top-hat," he said. He was fascinated by the tape machine in the office, but shied at the suggestion of visiting the Stock Exchange, saying that he could not bear the crowd. He said that he looked upon stockbroking as a profession of deep mystery in which great sums of money were made and lost overnight. But Mr. Gledhill noticed that he was quick to grasp the essential facts of business. This was clear when he produced the illustrations for the book.

One of his drawings illustrates the difference between a debenture, a preference share, a cumulative preference share, and a non-cumulative preference share. Two pairs of boys are each robbing a bird's nest up a tree. The first boy, walking away with four or five eggs in a basket, is the debenture holder, content with his modest booty and a sense of security. The second boy, who is tipping out the eggs from the other nest, is the preference shareholder, collecting his eggs with little trouble, and the boy who is catching them from below is the cumulative preference shareholder, delighted at receiving dividends unpaid for years past. The fourth boy, who is up the second tree, is the non-cumulative preference shareholder. Two Heath Birds are attacking him; it is more difficult for him to collect his dividends, and he looks back at the cumulative preference shareholder with envy because he himself cannot claim dividends from the past.

This shows how neatly he could express ideas which must have been completely foreign to him. Mr. Gledhill possesses another drawing which Heath did for him. As most people know, when a broker approaches a jobber for a price quotation, he does not say whether he is a buyer or a seller. Heath shows a crafty-looking jobber winding a handle which lowers a small bedroom mirror behind the top-hatted broker's back so that he can read the papers which he is cautiously holding behind him!

Heath Robinson's own venture into Big Business was a children's game, which sold well. But better than this were the games and gadgets, suitable for Christmas presents, which existed only in his imagination. The most famous of these was the Perimanicula, which was something like a penknife and which contained the following appliances: a gold pointer for pointing out on the timetable the trains you wished to catch, and a lead pointer for pointing out the trains you didn't wish to catch; a small spoon for administering medicine to sick birds, and a pair of tweezers for removing grit from sandwiches when on picnics!

Another was the Camel-hair Creave, for removing gravy stains from gravel paths. There were also games, such as the Set of Grilges, the object of which was to throw the Grilge as *short* a distance as possible; and the Fremmle Stick, which was stuck into the ground and round which the players had to walk as many times as they could. The more expensive model had an ivory knob which unscrewed to reveal a pencil and a pad for keeping the score.

There is no record that any of these surrealist games were ever played in the family. The sort of games which Heath liked best were those like Lexicon which gave him opportunities for the sort of foolery he enjoyed. With perfect gravity he would insist on some fantastic spelling of a word and justify it with logic which nobody could refute. There was always uproarious fun at his parties, although he himself was invariably quiet. Some-times his brothers, Tom and Charles, would be among the guests.

In 1937 Charles died. Heath said of him: " There was always something of youth and being on a holiday about Charles." He was not quite so reticent as his brothers. A great talker and a hard worker, with a cigar-ette dangling perpetually from the corner of his mouth, he had no difficulty in talking, working and smoking all at the same time.

Many stories are told about him. Owing to the dark glasses which he wore he was once given a penny by a well-meaning old gentleman. He touched his hat and took it, and when a friend remonstrated with him he said: " Well, he enjoyed giving it me and I didn't want to hurt his feelings."

At the time when Heath was living near Crouch End the three brothers would go into shops where they were well known, and Charles would play a leading part in elaborate playacting, in which all three of them called one another by fanciful names and had the girls behind the counter helpless with laughter.

Charles's death was a shock to Heath Robinson. Some years before this there had been another shock. His son, Alan, converted to Roman Catholicism, had retired to the monastery of Prinknash in Gloucestershire.

Except in his youth, Heath had never been a church-goer, and at one time he was so much a freethinker that he doubted the value of baptism. Nevertheless, he had always been interested in religious matters and often discussed them with Tom. As he grew older he veered more and more away from the mechanical view of life in which everything is supposed to happen owing to the play of blind forces. He had a deep-rooted belief in the dignity of Man, and he distrusted Socialist doctrines and others which viewed mankind " in the flat." Once when discussing a book on Darwin with a friend he bristled up and protested that the scientists ignored something fundamental which none of them could explain. This something, he said, was Divine Direction. No one knew why things happened; they only knew that they did happen. He went on to say that once he had been frankly materialistic, but suddenly he had realized there was something else which he had not taken into account.

But when his son said that he wished to become a monk it was a great blow to him and he used every argument he could think of to persuade him against it. At last, realizing that he was in earnest, he argued no longer but tried his best to understand the miraculous pull of a religion which could induce a young man to give up the world. He read a great many books written from the Catholic point of view and he was impressed by them.

When his son went to the monastery he went down with him, and it was then that he saw that monks may be " ordinary people." The novice master suggested that Alan should write to him and ask him for a drawing especially for the novitiate. Heath was quite willing; he sent an amusing sketch in colour of the monks repairing the novitiate roof. This picture of the brethren, who are raised and lowered on pieces of knotted string amid a forest of " Heath Robinson " scaffolding, still hangs in the monastery, and a great many postcards of it have been sold at Prinknash.

Heath went again, and his wife went with him. They stayed at the " Royal William " near by, and soon came to know some of the other monks. Sometimes he was invited to lunch in the refectory.

" I do not think it would be exaggerating to say," writes Dom Basil (as Alan has now become), " that he again experienced that sense of unity with all the human family which was at the bottom of his sympathy for all things human, and the reason why his humorous art made such a universal appeal. . . . He confessed to me that his one regret was that when in the refectory, good manners prevented him from bringing out his sketchbook and adding to the notes of his romping children in Waterlow Park a few sketches of the brethren. As a matter of fact, I have found one or two quick sketches of little incidents of monastic life that had struck him."

Having accepted the hospitality of the monastery, he wished to make some return, and so he and his wife made their home in Southwood Avenue, Highgate (where they had now moved) an open house for any of the monks who might be in London. He also helped the monastery in other ways. When Prinknash was erected into an abbey, the first abbot, Dom Wilfrid Upson, discussed a scheme with Heath for raising funds for the new abbey which they wanted to build. Heath agreed to illustrate a booklet in black and white, with some coloured plates, on the lines of the " How To Do It " series. Unfortunately, owing to failing health, he was unable to carry out the plan, but at Prinknash there is a dummy booklet and two coloured plates which he finished.

In time he became reconciled to his son's new life, and he even said that he envied him. He was relieved when Alan, perhaps the most gifted of the family, was able to continue his artistic work. He was always interested in the various commissions which he was given— chiefly in stone carving for churches and ceramic work, in which he has specialized for the last few years.

Mrs. Heath Robinson became a convert to Roman Catholicism, and there is just a possibility that had he lived longer Heath might have become a convert, too.

" Catholicism," he said, " is a religion of light." He compared it to the background of a stained glass window, essentially bright, but modified by its colours. " Rationalism, on the other hand, starts all dark, and by a supreme effort illumines portions of itself like a Rembrandt painting."

But the chance of his conversion is strongly denied by some of those who knew him best. In their opinion his love of the common people was too great for him to swallow the doctrine of Original Sin, and he was too much of an individualist to accept the dogmas and discipline of any orthodox religion.

CHAPTER XXI

ON TOP OF HIS WORLD IN BOTH WARS

AN acute observer once wrote that a man begins to grow old when he becomes condescending towards Youth. Heath Robinson was never condescending towards anyone. Some of his greatest friends were very young men, and if they happened to be artists he would take enormous trouble to help them with their work. He was particularly fond of young men who were lively and who responded to his wit. For one young artist he invented a ludicrous fiancée who was knockkneed, crosseyed and who bore the romantic name of Ratchett. A letter which he wrote to this young artist's brother after staying with the family in Wales shows how young at heart he remained to the end of his life.

" My dear Guy," he wrote, "this is a very hurried note, not in my usual classical style, to accompany the enclosed which I brought away with me, thinking that it was Alan's letter to his mother. Please pardon this characteristic mistake of mine, due no doubt to the hurry, or rather flurry of my departure.

" We had a good journey home. . . . For fellow passengers we had a real engine driver and his fireman who soon got into conversion with us—the engine driver with Tom and the fireman with me. . . . The fireman and I discussed Thomas and Sociology, the industrial position in this country, etc., etc.

" What a great time we had at Cwm zog ! I have been

trying to prolong the good time by repainting one of my sketches. . . .

" P.S. Do not think that Tom and I travelled on the engine. The driver and his stoker were returning from their weekend's rest after having taken a train to the country."

A curious thing about this holiday in Wales was that it was the first time Heath had ever seen a mountain.

To a younger artist whom he had befriended in his earlier days and who wrote to him in 1939, he replied, from his home in Southwood Avenue: " Since reading your elegant effusion, which incidentally thrilled me with its literary style, I have been searching in the caves of memory. I seem to remember in the days of my youth meeting with one, John Pelham Napper, a tall, handsome lad, whose eyes were alight with the flame of genius, on the Hill of Twenty Shepherds at Highgate. Have I the pleasure of addressing him? Also I call to mind a graceful nymph from the sunny woods of Surrey standing staunchly by his side. Do tell me if my memory plays me false; but I should be precipitated into the depths of despondency were the delightful vision dispelled from my mind. It is such dreams—am I not right, Mr. Napper?—that gild our riper years and make possible any kind of happiness during the sad times in which we live. These and the hope your letter holds out, of the realization once more of the pleasant dream of your presence in our neighbourhood, are among the few things that induce me to cling still to this existence.

" My best efforts—modest ones I admit—I continue to put forth for the benefit of my country, as you have noted. I regret these have not as yet met with that acclaim I had anticipated. I say ' as yet ' advisedly. You will find it difficult to believe that not one of my suggestions for carrying on and speedily ending this

TWELFTH NIGHT, ACT II, SCENE II. (*Hodder & Stoughton*)

disastrous war victoriously for ourselves has been adopted by the War Office. . . .

" Our own path is rough enough and likely to be rougher still, I fear, but we use our best endeavours to maintain our usual equable demeanour.

" You, too, I am sure, are doing this, you especially whom I can address in the words of the poet :

> ' My lovely English child
> My British, nay, nay,
> More than British, bouncing boy,
> Mine Empire laddy.' "

The second World War affected Heath, as it affected most men of innately peaceable disposition, with a sense of weariness and of the futility of human endeavour; but he rose gallantly to the occasion, and for the second time his caricatures of the War Machine appeared in dozens of journals to relieve civilian despondency and strengthen the morale of the troops.

In *Heath Robinson at War*, a book of his war cartoons published by Methuen in 1942, there are some fanciful methods of combating a Nazi invasion. When a German tank stops outside the " King's Head " and an unsuspecting member of the crew takes from the serving hatch a tankard of ale, ponderous wheels and ratchets are set in motion which lower the inn sign, with a small attached bomb, into the tank's open turret. Arriving at the cliffs of Dover an invading force sees holidaymakers in deck chairs, a beach band, paddlers and others, all apparently on dry land or in shallows, but in reality standing on piles; and jumping confidently from their landing craft they are drowned in the deep water. Enemy parachutists thinly disguised as visiting clergymen and the like are neatly caught by a special squad, in tubs, hipbaths and other receptacles filled with boiling water which are fitted in front of their bicycles. In the desert, a party of Blackshirts advances eagerly towards a group of tables loaded with bottles of wine beneath palm trees dangling bunches of tropical fruit secured by lengths of knotted string and on the tops of which roost squads of Tommies. But underneath this unexpected oasis is shown an enormous subterranean net with a lid worked by a concertina attachment, into which the Blackshirts will certainly fall. Flotillas of spherical man-carrying buoys, which spray seawater over small lumps of ice, lower the temperature of the Gulf Stream to such a point that the crew of a U-boat seen below surface are immobilized, and can only think of how to keep themselves warm. There are smaller sketches of a German stormtrooper armed with a bow and arrow cunningly camouflaged as a rifle, of a new piano-carrying tank for camp concerts, and of tin hats crowned with the heads and necks of water fowl so that in swimming across a river a platoon can pass for a hatch of ducks.

Some of his inventions for the Home Front are still more ingenious. There is an extraordinary contraption of chains, cranks and pulleys whereby an incendiary bomb can be extinguished without the bother of getting out of bed; and the roof-spotter's job is facilitated by a nightmare contrivance of windmills and revolving shafts, with a neat device which drops a weight on to an enormous concertina connected to a series of horns in the upper rooms of a general stores. The mounting economies of the nineteenforties are met by a new method of making austerity brides' cakes by plastering dough over canaries' cages, and a bashful gentleman taking his morning meal is startled by the appearance of a lady guest who has spent the night under his breakfast table. He draws a self-registering belt-tightener, shrapnel trousers for air raid wardens, and a legitimate method of stretching the tripe ration under the garden roller.

As in the first World War, suggestions for war cartoons were sent to him from all parts of the world. One which reached him from India ran:

"My small son, Peter, aged eleven, is constantly exercising his mind with ways and means of destroying That Man. Being an admirer of your genius (as my father, A. Bruce-Joy, the sculptor, was before me), I offer you Peter's latest war effort. . . .

"Peter says for the war to be won we shall need a sufficiency of troop-carrying and bomber aircraft, and some fighters, too. Also a large number of hungry tigers will be required. . . .

"Having fitted to each tiger a parachute having an automatic ripcord, load the tigers into the troop-carrier planes and proceed to the attack. . . . When the formation is over the enemy objective, release the tigers, which will float down onto the latter. During the floating process the tigers are to be wounded by skilful fire from our fighter planes, so that they may be out for blood when they land. . . ."

Writing to a friend in Canada in the forties, he said: "All the younger men and women are now being called up for war service of some kind and the veterans are taking their places in civilian life, so perhaps when I write to you next I shall be a butcher, or perhaps a house agent, unless I am fortunate enough to be made the manager of a public house. . . .

"We have one small joint of meat a week, but my wife has a genius for coaxing it through the seven days, assisted by vegetables. On Monday we have it warmed up, on Tuesday it is stewed, on Wednesday curried, on Thursday minced, and it finally fades away on Friday and Saturday in nourishing soups. . . .

"Tobacco is a difficulty and a barely excusable extravagance which I have not had the strength to forgo, but I expect I shall have to do so before long. It is sad to reflect that when our lives and characters are finally summed up, we shall have no credit for giving up those vices which we avoid only because we cannot indulge them, at least I suppose so.

" Here am I leading very nearly a blameless life and there are many in the same position. Smoking less than usual and perhaps not at all before long. Alcoholic indulgences reduced to a minimum. Never out late at night—it is not worth it in the blackout—and rising with the lark in the summertime when we alter our clocks. In fact, we lead lives of great temperance and restraint without credit for our self-denial."

With three sons in the Forces, failing health and all the anxiety and weariness of the war upon him, he must have found it hard to remain cheerful; yet he succeeded. When " Lord Haw-Haw " mentioned him in a broadcast, he chuckled and said that he had achieved real fame at last. Anxious for others, he was never nervous for himself. All through the early part of the war he kept up his gay old foolery. Calling at a young friend's house one day when spirits were low on account of the air raids, he announced himself as " Mr. Heath Robinson, the celebrated cartoonist," and another time he arrived at the house crowned with a colander! When this friend's house was bombed, he at once took in the whole family and never once complained of the discomfort which it caused him.

To Mr. Evans he wrote in December, 1940: ". . . I am holding the fort here not as a Home Guard, an A.R.P. Warden, an Auxiliary Fireman, or a Fifth Columnist, but as a little of all of them except the last. Quite unofficially I am told that my aim with the stirrup-pump could not be excelled even by William Tell. Fortunately as yet I have not been compelled to give any public demonstration. The technique of my blacking out is much admired in the neighbourhood and is the despair of Hitler."

A columnist who described him as walking on Hampstead Heath " with the air of a philosopher, which he is," remarked that few artists were at the top of their world in both wars. The Navy christened a cocktail after him—a cocktail which was a dash of everything, unorthodox but always exciting. Some people began to form the suspicion that he was a Mystery Man, a brilliant inventor who perversely chose to wear the cap and bells.

An opthalmic surgeon wrote to him about a picture of his which had appeared in *The Sketch* in 1944. " I feel sure you will be interested to learn that similar ideas were current at the time," he said. " A provisional patent bomb-detector was taken out by me in 1940 and submitted to the Ministry of Home Security. Although two large firms were ready to manufacture it, the Government would not allow licences to release the material. The idea was always called a ' Heath Robinson invention,' and apparently it was. I still think that if the Government had taken up the idea, millions of pounds worth of property would have been saved."

One day Heath received a mysterious invitation to lunch with a colonel from the War Office. In the course of the meal he was closely questioned as to where he had got his information for another drawing of his which had recently appeared. He replied that he had imagined it, but his host was still suspicious and continued to question him. He hinted at a grave leakage of top secret information. Apparently Heath Robinson's imagination was one jump ahead of the cleverest scientific brains of the day !

The war dragged on. A few years before, when a Press reporter had asked him for his views on old age,

Heath said: "It all depends upon what 'old age' means. If it means *sans* everything—in spite of the assistance of ear specialists, eye specialists, dentists, doctors, and other specialists, to check the inevitable progress—then all I would ask is a seat in the sun outside some country inn. That and a pipe and what contemplation I should be capable of. But I should much prefer to go on as I am, only more so."

Plenty of work still came his way, and even proposals for work in new directions. A suggestion was made to him that he should try his hand at animated cartoons. To this he replied that he had gone into the idea some years previously and had found it economically impossible. A factory would have to be hired and a staff of draughtsmen trained; a good deal of capital would be needed, and at least a year would pass before any money came in, during which time he would have to give up his ordinary work. He thought there were great possibilities in the idea, but not in the Disney tradition which was better left to Disney himself.

He also mentioned that he was getting on well with the new book. This was a collection of fairy tales written by Dr. Liliane Clopet which he was illustrating, and which appeared in 1944 under the title *Once Upon a Time* (Müller).

Dr. Clopet was delighted with his drawings and wanted him to illustrate a second book of hers, but Heath wrote, in August, 1944: ". . . I have to go into hopital for an operation, after which I shall need some time to recuperate, so that you see I shall not be able to undertake anything for some little time. Moreover, I have many arrears of work to make up before I undertake anything new."

By this time he was a very sick man. The operation was successful, but a relapse followed and on September 13th, he died.

The Press seized upon the modest sum which he left in his will to make a news feature of the event. How was it, they asked, that an artist of international fame should die almost in " poverty "? The answer is that Heath made no attempt to lay up for himself treasure upon earth : he earned considerable sums, but he spent them on his family. For himself he scarcely felt the need of money at all. He believed more in friends than in bank balances, and the enormous number of letters of condolence which were written to his widow showed how deeply his death was felt. Nearly everyone who met him liked him, and it is said that he had no enemies at all.

A memorial exhibition of his drawings was held by the Fine Art Society in February, 1945. In a preface to the catalogue, Mr. A. C. R. Carter, the well-known art critic, said :

" Equipped with abnormal powers of interpretation and of draughtsmanship, William Heath Robinson elected to devote his gifts to the invention of a new form of humour and laughter in art. He thereby created a truly comic and comforting relief to a machine-wearied and tormented world. He greased the monotonous wheels of toil by his elaborate fantasies. If Jules Verne were still with us, he would take fresh ideas from Robinson's flights of imagination. For myself I feel that beneath some of these drawings of miraculous mechanical impossibilities there must be lurking suggestions to those scientists for ever searching out the solution of some baffling problem. Such are those who ' laugh last.'. . .

" As one of the oldest chroniclers I have the duty of proclaiming that in William Heath Robinson the art world has lost one of the greatest black-and-white illustrators in the annals of art. . . . I recall the display in 1887 of Hugh Thomson's exquisite drawings for *Sir*

Roger de Coverley. Early in his career, Robinson bade fair to follow in his steps. His illustrations to *Twelfth Night* in this show prove it. I could wish that room could have been found for some of Robinson's weirdly interpretative drawings for the poems of Edgar Allan Poe. In these Robinson rivalled Aubrey Beardsley in his masterly nuances of line and imagination. Robinson was three months older than Beardsley; both being born in 1872.

" Phil May, whom I knew when we were both sixteen (in 1880) told me later that he greatly admired Robinson's gifts of ' serious illustration.'

" Yet, as already remarked, Robinson elected to put ambition aside. He was like that very rare type of actor —one who could play Hamlet but chose to become a Grimaldi."

CHAPTER XXII

HEATH ROBINSON'S PLACE AS AN ARTIST

THERE was a picture called " The Christening Party " on which Heath Robinson spent many months of his time and which he considered his best work. It hung in his studio, and once he told a friend that he would rather sell his clothes than part with it. The picture, which shows a party of people in gay clothes against a background of two flowering chestnut trees, one white and one pink, brings to a focus all the skill in the balancing of pattern and the subtlety of colouring which Heath Robinson had acquired in his fifty-odd years of experience.

Had he lived in earlier days, some rich patron of the Arts would have made it possible for him to follow his bent; as it was, he had to support a large family, and economic necessity compelled him to devote most of his time to Heath Robinson absurdities. He never complained, but he must have been aware that his public, although most enthusiastic, did not give him credit for the skill and craftsmanship which he put into even the lightest of his conceits. Most people were so tickled with the subjects of his drawings that they did not stop to consider the real secret of his success, which was the soundness of his work as a " serious artist." To the unthinking many he was a " funny man," and he became so identified with ridiculous contraptions that they hardly realized the quality of his achievement.

Even in his early days when he was learning as he went

along, there were clear signs of that peculiar imagination, decorative flair and considered balancing of detail which belong to every artist who is worth his salt. How quickly he developed these capacities may be seen by comparing his illustrations for the *Hans Andersen Fairy Tales* in the three editions published in 1897, 1899 and 1913. In the first, although there is plenty of fanciful imagination the faults are only too obvious. His children's faces are those of dummies, there is a lack of boldness, and in some cases the details are so fussy that they are trying to the eyes. In his picture of the boy busied among the icy fragments in " The Snow Queen," the cross-hatching gives a very wooden effect and the lumps of ice are like pieces of metal.

In his second attempt two years later, he is rather overshadowed by his brothers, Tom and Charles, who were more expert and assured; but his goblins are good, and there is a great sense of movement in his picture of Hans Clodhopper riding a ram with big horns, holding a cockerel, and with geese in the background.

But in the Hans Andersen published fourteen years later he has improved out of all belief. His drawings, particularly his coloured plates, are as delicate as soap bubbles. Looking at Tommalise riding on a swallow's back, or at the little mermaid soaring high above the rosy cloud with a precipitous island in the background, one feels almost airborne. Fascinating are the pearls round the Court Preacher's neck and the flowers in the kitchenmaid's hair in " The Nightingale." Looking at the picture of the storks and the sphinx in " The March King's Daughter " it is almost possible to feel the intense heat of the desert, though this is not an illustration in colour.

Heath Robinson acquired a special technique somewhat like Dulac's, for creating a faery effect by modulated lighting picked out with coloured points of light in beads, flowers, berries, water ripples, and so forth. In Kingsley's *Water Babies,* which he illustrated in 1915, there is an attractive picture of Tom looking at a dragonfly. Here the low-light is the brown pool in which he kneels, and the bright points are the coloured scales on the dragonfly's body, the intense blue of the pool's ripples, and the brilliant berries on a tree. There are submarine pictures with pin-points of light in the children's necklaces and hair-beads, and with extraordinary decorative effect and feeling of movement in the fishes which sport with them in the depths.

Similar characteristics stand out in his illustrations of *Twelfth Night* and *A Midsummer Night's Dream.* Dim woods with the eerie suggestion of sprites and goblins, moonlit fountains, the close inter-connection of Man and organic life—these are all components of the spell which catches and holds us fast. In some of his best illustrative work there is also a quality of colouring and a clarity of definition which springs from the influence of the Italian school. This is strange in a man who was intensely Saxon and who had nothing Latin in his temperament. The painters for whom he admitted admiration were Constable, Sickert and Steer.

In a different line are his drawings for the Edgar Allan Poe poems published in 1900. Here the highly ornate Beardsley technique is obvious and perhaps the influence of Walter Crane. Three years earlier he had done sixteen illustrations for an edition of *Don Quixote,* published by Bliss, Sands, and once again a comparison of these with his drawings for a later edition of *Don Quixote,* published by J. M. Dent in 1902, shows how rapidly he was developing yet another side of his talent. The first effort is a halting experiment. In the second he is still experimenting, but with marvellous assurance and success. The drawings are gay, unequal, full of versatility and inventiveness. It is the work of a young man aware of his growing powers, throwing himself with zest into his task, trying pencil and pen, this method and that, obviously enjoying himself. Sometimes he lapses into an earlier, more immature style—as for instance in his stilted drawing of Don Quixote on the enchanted bark, with Sancho Panza weeping, and in his unattractive portrayal of Dorothea. (He never could draw a well-dressed lady.) But in such pictures as Sancho listening with great attention to his master, and the bespectacled Donna Rodriguez sitting by Don Quixote's bed, the delicacy of his line and the expert manipulation of his masses of black and white are truly remarkable.

He was always happy with bizarre figures, and in his illustrations of Rabelais, which he did in 1913, he found expression for another side of his talent. This was a task of his own seeking and once again it shows an unexpected streak in a man who led a life so apparently dull, one might almost say suburban. Rabelais is wild, coarse, exuberant; he is the medieval jester of French literature, the clown who saw the world as clownish. For an artist he is overwhelming in the wealth of material which pours from his pen. To pick something out of that tawny spate is like trying to catch Niagara in a teaspoon. The force of the torrent is enough to stultify the brain, and in the days when Heath Robinson was commisioned to do the drawings, there was the danger that a too faithful interpretation might send the reading public into a swoon. A French illustrator of Rabelais whose drawings were exhibited in London had his collection seized and taken off to Bow Street, where an outraged magistrate ordered its immediate destruction on the grounds of indecency! Hedged about with these restrictions, Heath made a bold and on the whole very successful attempt. He drew his originals on a large scale which made possible a broad treatment of the

—*Rabelais (Navarre Society)*

subject. His drawings were different from those of Doré, Pape, Chalons and other French illustrators of Rabelais. His types are so bizarre that they are scarcely human. Yet the distortions are based on observable human traits, and the " overload " is quite legitimate. In these drawings Heath Robinson comes near to being ferocious. They show that he could be a merciless critic.

Yet another distinct line of creative work is shown in his illustrations of Kipling's *A Song of the English*. Here the feelings are of patriotism, the soldier's Hereafter, the Guardian Seas of England, the Spirit of Empire. Heath Robinson's versatility was never more

—*Rabelais (Navarre Society)*

clearly apparent than in his coloured drawings of soldiers, half awake, half asleep, watching the ghostly march of hosts and the passing of ships.

His versatility did not stop short at human beings and half-human caricatures; he had a wonderful gift for drawing animals. As a young man of twenty-five he showed what he could do when he illustrated *The*

—*Rabelais (Navarre Society)*

Giant Crab. In this book alone are pictures of young elephants, a hypocritical cat, rats, a crocodile and a monkey, a boar, a wise and a foolish parrot, a mouse, a crane, fish, a jackal, a falcon, a lion and some geese; and in his illustrations of subsequent books, such as *The Talking Thrush*, *Peacock Pie* and *Topsy-Turvy Tales*, he passes with ease to a great many other species, all of

—*Rabelais (Navarre Society)*

which are drawn with a sureness of touch that expresses the essential nature of the beast. Often these animals are very much as they would appear to the imagination of a child. In Perrault's *Old Time Stories* the horrifying Beast gloriously attired to court the Beauty is just the sort of figure which might appear in childish nightmares, while the enormous brilliant green frogs in the *Friendly Frog* story are no doubt as frogs would look to a young child who sees the world magnified and unmarred by the sooty incrustations of time.

When Heath Robinson's well-known humorous work is added to the total, it will be clear that he possessed not one reputation as an artist but half a dozen. Too much versatility is a dangerous gift unless there is some unifying principle behind it, since it may easily dissipate an artist's creative force and make him a jack of all trades. The question arises, then, was there some essential quality which entered into each of these different styles of his work, some main stem as it were from which each of them sprang?

At first sight there is nothing which unites the macabre interpretations of Poe's poems, the coarse buffoonery of the Rabelais drawings, the delicate fantasy of his fairy tale illustrations and Shakespeare fantasies, and the ludicrous pomposity of his Heath Robinson contraptions. But if we look a little closer we shall see some connecting threads. No matter how seemingly trivial or absurd his subject, he never lost his sense of artistic responsibility; though he might play the fool with ideas, he never played the fool with art. Indeed, it was his strict observance of the rules of art— his considered spacing and balancing and his pains-taking manipulation of detail and design — which enabled him to play the fool so effectively. An audience is always aware when a lecturer knows his subject, and for this reason they will listen to him with respect. All of us who look at a Heath Robinson drawing know beyond any doubt that the artist has mastered his technique, and because of this the picture, however absurd in its conception, acquires pictorial authority. It compels us to take it seriously, no matter whether it be some delicate fantasy or an utterly impossible Heath Robinson invention which our reason tells us could never belong to the world of sanity.

In much of his work, though not all of it, this pictorial authority goes hand in hand with something else which belongs partly to childhood and partly to the state which is half way between dreams and awakening. This is a sort of incongruous naïveté, solemnly insisted upon and

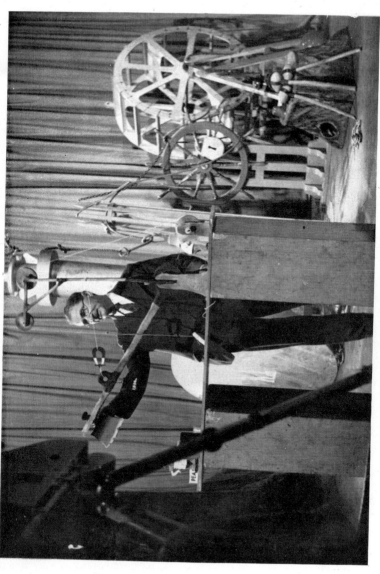

HEATH ROBINSON WITH HIS OWN MODEL OF A PEA-SPLITTING MACHINE

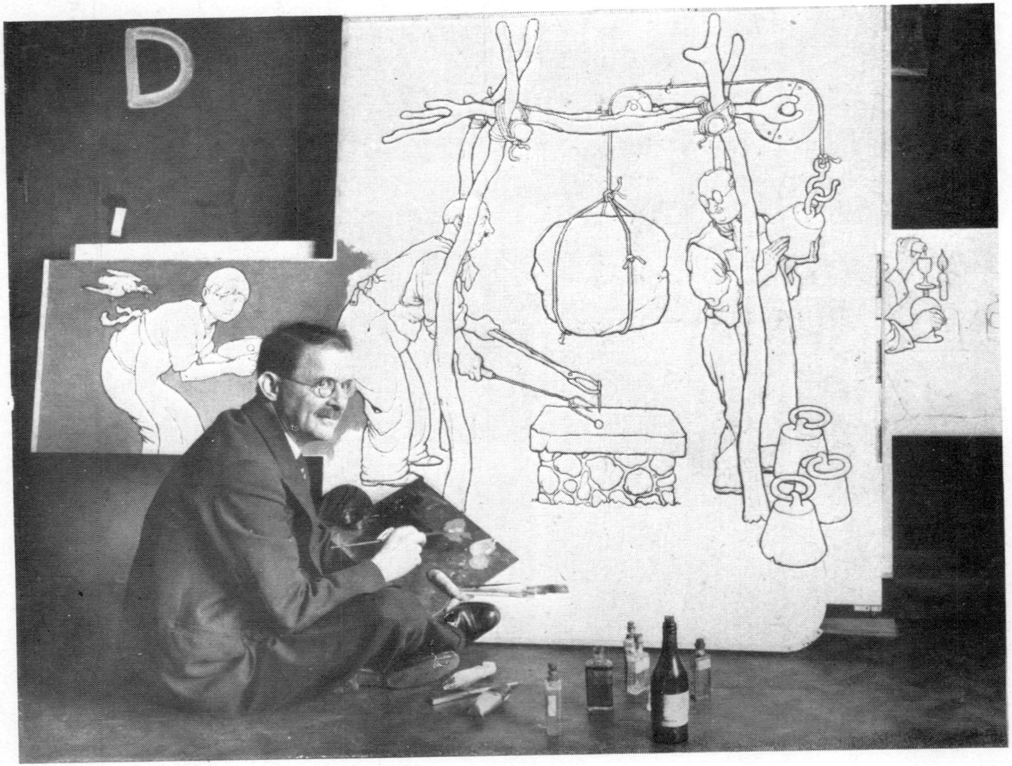

HEATH ROBINSON DRAWING FOR TELEVISION

backed by a curious Heath Robinson logic. Most of us have seen a young child engrossed in the solemn manner of infants in a task which he cannot clearly grasp but which he feels certain will lead to some exciting result. Many of Heath Robinson's drawings have something of this in them; in fact this is the spirit which animates them. There is a slight eccentricity of outlook, a happy inconsequence, a disparity between means and ends which deflates the utilitarian view of the world.

This was essential to the man who was to caricature machinery. A machine is a cold, precise instrument which works within the rigid compass of its function, and the people of a machine age are always in danger of shaping their lives on a similar pattern. But nature is not like this; she is gay, lavish, experimental.

Heath realized this, and he hinted at it both directly and by a process of *reductio ad absurdum*.

CONCLUSION

A S I have tried to show, Heath Robinson became famous as a humorous artist in spite of himself. He wished to do serious illustration work, but the public insisted upon his drawings of crazy machinery and preposterous mechanical methods. Resigning himself to this, he tried merely to amuse, but while amusing he succeeded in doing something more: he caricatured machinery with such skill that he struck a blow at Machine Worship and enabled the machine-servers to laugh at their Frankenstein; and he skitted the disparity between ends and means in such a way that he exposed what is perhaps the most sinister trend in our present-day civilization.

Humanity has acquired the technical knowledge and the physical means to produce almost anything, but except on the surface human nature remains practically unaltered, so that we get little good out of applied science, and indeed considerable harm.

Take as an example the internal combustion engine. The law insisted upon the first motor cars being preceded by a man with a red flag. Perhaps this was a piece of unconscious prophetic dramatisation like the war trumpets of Pharaoh which after the lapse of 4,000 years were blown and broadcast from Cairo on the true opening of the second World War. By 1939 enormous numbers of motor cars congested the roads of Great Britain and the road casualties were greater than those caused by a modern war. Vast motor manufacturing firms had come into being, with cognate industries such as oil production, rubber growing and steel rolling which employed millions of men and amassed huge fortunes for the principal shareholders. Defoe would have rubbed his hands in satisfaction and put all this down on the credit side of the balance sheet. But is it as simple as this? How many men get more out of life by accumulating vast bank balances? How many workers are happier for working in a factory, a rubber plantation or an oilfield, drawing higher wages? In the Balkans you may still find peasants who are living under much the same conditions as our own peasantry lived in the Middle Ages. By modern standards their lives are extremely hard, yet, apart from distress caused by wars, you cannot help noticing their peculiar serenity and contentment. On gala occasions they are capable of the most vivid gaiety.

Like the salt-machine which ground salt and could not be stopped, the Industrial Machine continues to manufacture regardless of human happiness. In a few years' time motor cars will be pouring out of the factories in torrents swifter than ever. All of us will have to have a car. If we persist in cycling or going on foot, our best friends will have to tell us that our habits are uncivilized. Great new bypasses and speedways of blistering concrete will cut swaythes through the green heart of England, petrol-filling stations will spring up in hundreds of meadows like crops of fungi. And all for what? So that bigger and faster lorries may deliver greater quantities of raw materials to the factories to enable more mass-produced goods to be manufactured and forced upon (by that time) an over-stocked market; so that even more private motorists may speed down the Broad Way, like Goya's *chinchillas,* seeing nothing, hearing nothing, knowing nothing.

Or take Medicine. At one time we looked to human

beings to cure us of our illnesses, but now we look to the Machine. Vast chemical combines pour forth thousands of tons of drugs and remedies which are put on the market and swallowed, but would anyone be bold enough to say we are any the healthier for them?

" The mammoth organization of sick benefits and insurance likewise plays its part in the despiritualization of ill-health," writes Mr. Stefan Zweig, " and more and more tends to rob disease of individuality, so that a large-scale industry arises in the running of which there is never a moment's leisure for personal contact between physician and patient, and wherein there is no longer a trace of magnetic rapport between the soul of the healer and the soul of the healed. The family doctor is dying out. . . ."*

These illustrations could be multiplied indefinitely. Science has given us the Machine which, like the jinnee in the bottle, salaams and wishes to know our commands; but all we can think of asking for is something to make our lives more mechanical than before. Urban life is intensely mechanical, and so are the ponderous ramifications of finance. What is a business man but a man who is forever mechanically busy? What is a government servant but a man engrossed in the rules of governing and hardly concerned with sympathetic service?

As the Machine increases the complexity of life, so more and more government seems to be necessary. Bureaucracy, that perfect example of a Heath Robinson contraption, multiplies its cogwheels and ratchets, its pulleys and its strands of knotted string, until we are all caught up in it and involved in the ludicrous process of pea-splitting or whatever it may be, with venerable Whitehall officials perched on platforms owlishly

---

* *Mental Healers by Stefan Zweig (Cassell).*

gazing at watches, and top-hatted Cabinet Ministers standing solemnly by the controls.

The Heath Robinson machines which regulate our lives are not unnaturally subject to sudden and violent breakdowns. Our economic system, knocked together like Heath's first G.W.R. locomotive from the scrap-heap of outworn theories, can hardly be expected to suit the Power Age, however it may have worked in the days of handicraft. Except in abnormal times when demand outstrips supply it works badly enough, and when there is so-called " over-production " it barely fires on one cylinder. There is mass unemployment and wholesale bankruptcy, and we have to practise sabotage on a large scale to keep it going at all. Finally, after an uneasy period, another war breaks out. Once again the Machine-God is in his Heaven and all's wrong with the world.

In times of peace we are like children who have been given expensive presents unsuited to our age, but in wartime we are more like monkeys in a bomb factory. The disparity between means and ends is so patent that no one can now believe that any combatant gets something out of a war, or even that anyone " wins " it. Scientific knowledge is many lengths ahead of ethical development and is thundering up the straight. Atom bombs and warnings of forces even more deadly have shaken the disciples of Dr. Ure from their uneasy sleep.

It is not my purpose to attempt to analyse the causes of war or the cankers of peace, but only to show that the humorous work of Heath Robinson pointed, like the lead pointer of the Perimanicula, to the trains which we don't want to catch. At present we are in the wrong train: in a train which is taking us towards increased mechanization of human enterprise, of human society, even of individual human life. With an awful solemnity the crazy machinery has been set to work, and the results, however pitiful or catastrophic, are justified by all the arts of modern propaganda. In hundreds of drawings Heath Robinson gave us a graphic picture of the kind of machinery in which we are involved. He caricatured our mechanical tyrant and showed us its absurdity.

UNCLE LUBIN'S HOLIDAY

IN the nineteen-forties Heath Robinson began to write and illustrate a sequel to *Uncle Lubin* which he called *Uncle Lubin's Holiday*. In this book, which was never finished, Uncle Lubin has shed his tall hat and belted overcoat and become a respectable suburban father with a muffler and an umbrella. With his wife, Aunt Glamorgan, and his son, Peter, he decides to take a holiday in Margate, and charters a taxi from Mr. Bagtrot, a friendly taximan. But even before they get as far as Ludgate Hill they meet with astonishing adventures, and instead of arriving at Margate they find themselves in the Indian jungle.

Some of the characters have their origin in the bedtime stories which Heath Robinson told his own children, and some seem to be founded on well-known figures from real life. Willy Scrimmage, for instance, reappears as the son of the railway porter, while Mr. Bagtrot is a first cousin to Mr. Belchamber, of Cranleigh, who once transported the family to Bognor under adventurous circumstances.

THE STORY

ONE DAY Uncle Lubin said at breakfast : " Let's all go for a holiday." " Certainly," replied Aunt Glamorgan, " why not?" " Yes, let's," said Peter.

After much thought, Uncle Lubin said that Margate was the best place to go to. He had been there before

"HE HAD BEEN THERE BEFORE"

and knew what it was like.   So they all packed up and ordered a taxi.

Now there was only one taxi to be had, and that belonged to Mr. Bagtrot.   But he was a friend of the family and would drive them to the station all right and not charge them too much.

They had not gone very far when Uncle Lubin remembered that his hair wanted cutting, so they stopped at a barber's shop in a turning off the Strand, W.C.2.

It was a tumbledown kind of place, with ivy growing all over the front and across the doorway.   This didn't bother Uncle Lubin the least little bit.   He rubbed away the moss from the hinges of the door so that it should open more easily, and without any trouble he pushed his way through the ivy and got into the shop.

"IT WAS A TUMBLEDOWN KIND OF PLACE"

"THE BARBER WAS A CRAZY OLD MAN"

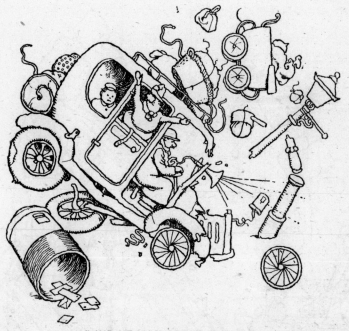

"AND NEARLY BROKE IN TWO"

The barber was a crazy old man, crippled with rheumatics. The shop was crazier and older still. Having your hair cut was a slow job. The old barber would leave off now and then to scrape away the lichen that had grown in the cracks of the washbasin or shuffle across the room to remove a cobweb, or to see if his traps had caught any mice. Again, he would slowly sharpen his razors on a toadstool which he had picked from the corner of the room where many were growing.

All of this fussing inside the shop took up a lot of time, and Mr. Bagtrot became impatient. He sounded his horn rather gently at first to remind Uncle Lubin in case he had forgotten them.

At last he almost lost his temper, and gave such a shattering blast on his horn that the taxi was lifted right

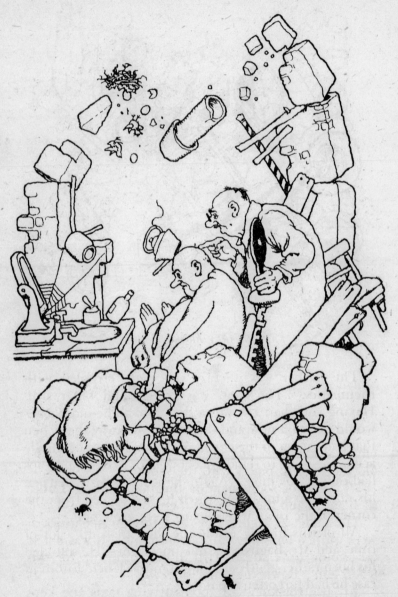

"THE OLD SHOP FELL TO PIECES WITH THE SHOCK"

"MR. BAGTROT SOON MENDED THE TAXI"

off its hind wheels and nearly broke in two, while the old shop fell to pieces with the shock.

Mr. Bagtrot soon mended the taxi. Uncle Lubin then got in and they went on their way.

The taxi was a good one, and though not quick it went quite a long way without stopping. It was not so easy going up Ludgate Hill, but it made up for this when going down the other side.

Mr. Bagtrot knew all about driving taxis and kept a book of the rules by his side in case he forgot any of them, so at last they arrived at the station without many accidents on the way.

Having bought the tickets, they went on the platform, sat down and waited. There was no train in just then.

When they had been there for an hour and seventeen minutes, Uncle Lubin began to fidget, so they called at the office of the station master and asked him when the train for Margate was expected. He told them that it

" *WITHOUT MANY ACCIDENTS ON THE WAY* " (rough drawing)

"A GREAT SAVING IN MATCHES" (rough drawing)

had left three hours ago. They were very cross on hearing this. Uncle Lubin asked him if he had any more trains. The station master replied, " Only a few specials in the yard, come and choose one," which was certainly very kind of him.

When Uncle Lubin had chosen the train, it was

brought round to the platform. Before they got in, the station master introduced them all to the engine driver, who seemed a cheerful and reliable man. They had only travelled three-quarters of a mile when Uncle Lubin wished that he had chosen a quicker train. "You can never tell how quick a train is from the outside," he remarked.

But this had one advantage, the engine driver, who was a great smoker, was able, when driving at night, to get out without stopping the train, to climb up a signal and light his pipe at the candle in the lantern and then easily to catch up with the train before it had gone too far. This was a great saving in matches.

Presently they entered a tunnel and the train went slower and slower until it stopped. It was very dark and they could hear the driver hammering away and talking to himself.

In a little while he walked down the train to their carriage and explained to Uncle Lubin that the screw, which holds the piston rod to the under-side of the valve which connects the boiler with the flywheel, had worked loose and fallen into the boiler. He had been trying to fish it out with a hammer but it was no use, so he would have to seek some further help. He then walked off through the tunnel and they waited patiently in the darkness.

Help came at length and the train was hauled through the tunnel to a little wayside station at the other end, where they were glad to alight.

The rest of this unfinished story is indicated by the author's own synopsis which follows :

CHAPTER 4.—THE AEROPLANE

The travellers are taken by the ticket collector to the house of William Scrimmage (the son of the porter). Willie Scrimmage has made an aeroplane in his back garden. They decide to continue their journey to Margate in the plane. Arriving over Margate, they cannot make it come down. The plane drifts over the sea, and they finally find themselves over the jungle in India. They land by parachute. The empty plane drifts away.

CHAPTER 5.—THE JUNGLE

The travellers (now consisting of Uncle Lubin, Aunt Glamorgan, Peter, the ticket collector, the porter and his son, Willie Scrimmage) hunt animals with ingenious apparatus invented by Uncle Lubin on the spot.

CHAPTER 6.—THE RAJAH

The party is captured by an Eastern potentate whose indignation at their trespass is soon appeased on his realizing the good intentions of his captives. He is the richest potentate on earth, because of the numerous wedding presents he receives on the occasion of his many weddings.

CHAPTER 7.—THE GOLDEN PEG TOP

Strange affair of heir to the throne. His melancholy. Cause discovered. Has lost golden peg top in Persian Gulf.

CHAPTER 8.—THE SUBMARINE

Uncle Lubin and party construct a submarine to search depths of sea for the golden peg top. Eventually they discover a merman spinning the peg top with an eel. Peg top taken from merman by guile or bargain.

CHAPTER 9.—THE NORTH POLE

On their way back to the potentate's palace, they lose their way and find themselves beneath the ice at the North Pole. Adventures at the North Pole. Icebergs, polar bears, etc.

CHAPTER 10.—THE DESERT ISLAND

Continuing their journey under the sea, they come to the surface near a desert island. Adventures thereon.

CHAPTER 11.—THE DUGONG

CHAPTER 12.—THE RETURN

Volcano on desert island. Crater. Caves. Subterranean journey through underground passages. After a journey of some months, passage leads into tube railway. They all come out into Ludgate Hill once more, via escalator. Mr. Bagtrot happens to be in the station yard at the time and joyfully invites Uncle Lubin, Aunt Glamorgan and Peter inside. Taxi. The whole procession, which now consists of Uncle Lubin, Aunt Glamorgan and Peter in Mr. Bagtrot's taxi, the rajah on his elephant, the prince, the merman, the dugong, the ticket collector, the porter and Willie Scrimmage, his son, now proceed up Fleet Street. Reporters crowd the pavements, taking notes for their newspapers.

TAILPIECE

Homecoming celebrations, feast to all, and end of Uncle Lubin's holiday.

TRIBUTES TO W. HEATH ROBINSON

The following appreciations of the work of W. Heath Robinson by distinguished men in various walks of life have been written specially for this volume. They are evidence of the lively impression which he made on his contemporaries.

MAJOR-GENERAL IAN HAY BEITH (Ian Hay).

My recollections of Heath Robinson's delightful nonsense are a bit vague now, though I do remember the cheering effect upon troops in the trenches of his series of war-winning machines—tied up with string!

The odd thing about these contraptions was that if you studied them really closely, there seemed to be no particular reason why they should not work. At the back of it all, he must have had the mind of a constructional engineer.

The picture of his which I shall always remember came out, I think, in *The Sketch,* about Christmas, 1915. It was a picture of the interior of a trench, with a row of British soldiers sleeping, each with his Christmas stocking hung up above his head. A spectacled German soldier, very inadequately disguised as Father Christmas, was creeping along the parapet, placing a bomb in each stocking.

SIR HAROLD BELLMAN.

I think the supreme merit of Heath Robinson's work was that he made us laugh at our adaptations and improvizations and brought a new vein of humour to the art of the caricaturist. His was a new and novel technique, and in this sphere he had no peer.

To record my warm appreciation is to acknowledge, but not to discharge indebtedness to him for many a hearty laugh. I do not think it is just stupid insularity which makes me feel that no other country could produce a Heath Robinson. It isn't given to many other countries to have that peculiar sense of humour which revels in a joke against oneself.

NICOLAS BENTLEY.

How seldom do we find united in one intellect an equal mastery of both scientific and æsthetic principles? There springs to mind, of course, the example of Da Vinci. But for a comparable genius between the Renaissance and the twentieth century we seek almost in vain. Almost, until we come upon Heath Robinson, who, I venture to say, had the advantage of Leonardo, in that some of his inventions did at least *look* as if they might have worked. Even the fact that there was usually a much simpler method of achievement than the Heath Robinson method does not detract from the satisfaction of being able to see exactly how the invention might have worked. Nor is this due alone to the simplicity of Robinsonian logic; even with his passion for detail, Heath Robinson always remained explicit, always economical. His drawings were composed with a care and ingenuity which reminds one, in the more elaborate illustrations, of Doré; at other times, in the bold yet subtle disposition of blacks and whites, they are reminiscent of Beardsley.

Some may think it a pity that Heath Robinson should have abandoned his earlier and more serious *métier*; in particular his illustrations for children's books. This is not to decry his later work, but to lament that drawings in his earlier manner are so seldom to be seen. Yet if he had persisted in this, perhaps we should never have had the kind of illustration that is to be described only as " a Heath Robinson drawing." And without this the rare tradition of English humorous art would certainly have been the poorer.

KENNETH BIRD (" Fougasse ").

It is always easier to diagnose the causes of failure than the causes of success, and that is why a reasoned appreciation of Heath Robinson is so difficult—he was so calmly and uniformly successful, both in his decorative compositions and in the so-called fantasies for which he is more widely known. I say " so-called fantasies," for in reality they were not fantastic in the least—which gives the clue, maybe, to the chief reason for their success.

In a world rapidly becoming more technical and more mass-produced, they symbolized, I think, the rebellion against the tyranny of the specialist and his standardized productions; they stood defiantly for free enterprise carried to the limit.

They showed us, in fact, the "little man in the street" in revolt against his machine-made age, determined to make his own world in his own way, and from the materials to be found in his own backyard and boxroom—and that is, I believe, one of the chief reasons why we enjoyed them.

His imitators, who concentrated on "funny" mechanical devices, naturally failed where he succeeded: his own mechanical devices weren't consciously "funny"—they were the devices that a defiant individualist would construct if he determined to do so without help or advice from anybody. That is, I think, why they *are* funny, naturally funny, intrinsically and inherently funny—funny for the best of all reasons, because human nature itself is funny.

The technical side of his art is, of course, of less general interest than the human side; I must, therefore, content myself with pointing out how well his art concealed its art, and how well it carried out and expressed his ideas, clearly, impersonally, dispassionately. In his decorative work, the trees never concealed the wood, nor did the wood conceal its component parts, the trees; in his humorous work every string and every knot in it, every pulley and every broomstick, was set out plainly and precisely, and without prejudice or favour.

Of the greatness of Heath Robinson there is no question— has not his name passed into the common currency of our language? It is now the recognized noun (noun of assembly, one might almost call it) for a mechanical makeshift, an amateur contraption of stick and string, and although, as I have tried to suggest, there was a very great deal more to it than that, at all events his fame is secure so long as string and stick and amateur mechanics remain.

Sir KENNETH CLARK.

Humour is much concerned with the grotesque application, or misapplication, of cause and effect. A shot is heard, and the comedian says: "My God, I'm poisoned." Heath Robinson applied this principle to a department of human effort which we hold in such awe that we usually do not consider it a suitable subject for jokes—to machinery. His machines all work perfectly. The chain of cause and effect is complete. Only, after we have followed it, we realize that what they do is quite unnecessary, or could have been done without machinery at all. There is a grotesque disproportion between means and ends; and at the back of our minds we know that these contraptions, which appear so logical, would not work at all, and that their logic is really that of a fairy tale. But there is just enough of the fantastic and improbable in real machinery to keep us in suspense on this point. If Heath Robinson's inventions were a fraction more fantastic we should lose interest in them. When I was studying Leonardo da Vinci's drawings in the Codice Atlantico, I was constantly reminded of Heath Robinson, for Leonardo was so enchanted by the ingenuity of his machines that he did not stop to inquire if they could be constructed, or were worth constructing. But they came at the beginning of the age of science, when machinery promised to be man's servant; whereas Heath Robinson lived in the age of science triumphant, when machinery had become a tyrant; and, as we all know, the man who ridicules tyrants is a champion of humanity.

PROFESSOR J. B. S. HALDANE.

About March, 1915, a machine for throwing hand grenades for a few hundred yards from British to German trenches appeared in France. It was immediately christened the "Heath Robinson Gun." Whether this title became official I do not know, but it certainly caught on.

I think the reason was that it was extremely cumbrous, but you could see exactly how it worked. This was, I think, the salient feature of Heath Robinson's drawings. I think they played a genuine part in educating my generation, and in driving home the fact that machines did a great deal more than merely work. Robinson's worked like Charlie Chaplin on a tightrope, almost collapsing at every movement.

By exposing their negative, Heath Robinson did something to further the principles of modern machine design, just as a caricaturist of the human species may promote virtue by caricaturing vice.

J. F. HORRABIN.

I first became an admirer of Heath Robinson's work forty years ago, when I was an art student. In those days he was doing those charming book illustrations, and one thought of him along with Rackham and Byam Shaw as a draughtsman with a lovely decorative sense. Then, later, he became Heath Robinson: an artist-humorist whose name could no longer be coupled with anyone else's; so highly individual a name, indeed, that it supplied a new word to contemporary colloquial language. Henceforth any mechanical contrivance, domestic or otherwise, which looked more ingenious than reliable was to the man in the street a " Heath Robinson contraption."

He repeated himself, superior persons said. So did every artist of strong individuality — Van Gogh or Raeburn, Rowlandson or Lautrec. He developed a style which exactly expressed both his own personality and his own peculiar humour. And both personality and humour were worth repeating!

I met him in the flesh only once—in the television studio at Alexandra Palace, where the tangle of cables and mikes and lamps and contraptions balanced on ladders provided a not inappropriate background. For once one was not disappointed at meeting one of one's heroes in the flesh. The quiet, twinkling little old gentleman seemed to me the perfect embodiment of what one had imagined the real Heath Robinson to be. And he looked happy—like a man who has really found his *métier* and knows he has expressed himself in it.

DR. C. E. M. JOAD.

Mr. Heath Robinson was the first draughtsman who had the sense to see the menace which lay in machines. Realizing as he did that most human beings now spend most of their lives in attendance upon these monsters, in giving them to eat and drink and in washing and generally servicing them, and in trying to keep them in a good temper; realizing, too, that they are in grave danger of superseding men as the next level of evolutionary development, as man, whom the animals evolved, has superseded them, Heath Robinson had the wit to deal with the situation by trying to laugh the machines out of court.

He actually had the audacity to make fun of the contemporary idol, even to " cock snooks " in its face.

I am afraid his campaign must be accounted a failure since the machines are still worshipped by the young, who think that sixty miles an hour is ten times as good as six miles an hour, that six hundred miles an hour is ten times as good as sixty miles an hour and that six thousand miles an hour is practically the same as heaven. Still, he did his best, a modern Don Quixote tilting at real windmills!

E. V. KNOX, Editor of *Punch*.

Like everybody else, I suppose, I used to be immensely amused by his mechanical complications, traced after so many stages to their simple and efficient ends, and I dare say he was the first black and white artist to burlesque the madness of modern machinery. I don't think he did more than one drawing for *Punch*. . . .

He certainly contributed to what used to be called the gaiety of nations in the days when nations still had some.

Lord NUFFIELD.

Heath Robinson was one of my pets, for although his mechanical schemes were perfectly ridiculous, they always produced the desired results in the most roundabout way.

He will be greatly missed, and it will be difficult to replace his particular type of humour.

J. B. PRIESTLEY.

I would certainly like to put in a word for Heath Robinson, who was not only an accomplished comic draughtsman but might be considered a pioneer in pictorial humour, because undoubtedly he anticipated a great deal of the characteristic humour of this machine age. Both here and in America among many successful comic artists you still see his influence at work.

Professor A. E. RICHARDSON, R.A.

MacHeath Robinson might be a good title for this ingenious caricaturist of machinery. Prior to his entering the lists, few had shown that machinery has personality and could be made ridiculous. It often happens that the concurrence of a period with the advent of a particular mentality produces very apposite results. Heath Robinson is a case in point. He saw quite clearly that most things in life are the outcome of hasty improvization, and that things tied up with string and held together by cotton reels have an interest which also belongs to the most intricate machinery.

His theory appears to have been that simple results were often achieved by laborious methods. Research among discarded blueprints and the outpourings of engineers' offices might well prove the theory of indefinite labour prior to successful achievement. In one sense Heath Robinson was a fantasist, in another he had the makings of a great inventor. His caricatures of men and contraptions never fail to set the mind at work to unravel the cobwebs of his facile invention. It is, for example, ludicrous to find a building suspended from skyhooks attached to balloons, or to study a decrepit steam roller driven by a tramp fulfilling the dual purpose of rolling a garden path and generating electricity for a prefabricated bungalow.

One often thought that Heath Robinson's strange interpretation of the human mind could be applied to the cumbersome workings of political machinery. The value of his drawings adheres in their impossibility, no less than in the deep satire which they imply. One cannot help feeling that the artist enjoyed creating these curious patterns of revolving wheels, hooks, balances and other improvisations. Nothing came amiss to his imaginative skill; frying pans, alarm clocks, trombones, bird cages and kites, embody all the attributes of the flying machine, for, if the inner workings of the most scientific machine should be disintegrated, a Heath Robinson effect would at once result.

I regard this great man as having given public service in bringing the force of his satire to bear on modern illusions. We need another such artist to deal with the cynicism which is the basis of modern art.

BERT THOMAS.

It falls to the lot of few of us to achieve the distinction of one's name becoming a " household word." The name " Heath Robinson " stands for everything of a crazy mechanical nature. Any weird contraption of nuts, bolts and pulleys is immediately dubbed as " Heath Robinson." This occurred continually during the last war and will, I feel sure, go on indefinitely.

This side of Heath Robinson's genius, which made him world famous, was only a part of his long life's output. His humorous illustrations, so individual in outlook, were a joy to his numerous admirers for many years. Personally, his book illustrating appealed to me most—in these he displayed an excellence of invention which was very satisfying. His *Twelfth Night* especially was a gem; and though he lacked the superb draughtsmanship of Rackham, there was a quality and charm in his illustrations of the classics that ensures his reputation as a serious artist.

I had the pleasure of his friendship for many years, and greatly admired him both as an artist and a man.

BOOKS ILLUSTRATED BY W. HEATH ROBINSON

Danish Fairy Tales and Legends of Hans Andersen. 16 illustrations. (Bliss Sands.) 1879.

Pilgrim's Progress. 24 illustrations. (Bliss Sands.) 1879, reissued 1908.

Don Quixote. 16 illustrations. (Bliss Sands.) 1897.

The Giant Crab and Other Tales from Old India, by W. H. D. Rouse. (David Nutt.) 1897.

The Arabian Nights. (Constable.) 1899, reissued 1908.

Danish Fairy Tales and Legends. Illustrated jointly with Tom and Charles Robinson. (Dent.) 1899.

The Talking Thrush, by W. Crook. (Dent.) 1899.

Poems of Edgar Allan Poe. (Bell.) 1900.

Tales from Shakespeare, by Charles Lamb. 16 illustrations. (Sands.) 1902.

Mediæval Stories, by J. H. E. Schück. (Sands.) 1902.

Don Quixote. (Dent.) 1902.

The Adventures of Uncle Lubin, by W. Heath Robinson. (Grant Richards.) 1902. (Chatto and Windus.) 1925.

The Child's Arabian Nights. (Grant Richards.) 1903.

Ramayána. Rama and the Monkeys. (Dent.) 1903.

Monarchs of Merry England, by R. Carse. (Fisher Unwin.) 1908.

Twelfth Night, by William Shakespeare. (Hodder & Stoughton.) 1908.

A Song of the English, by Rudyard Kipling. (Hodder & Stoughton.) 1909.

Bill the Minder, by W. Heath Robinson. (Constable.) 1912.

Hans Andersen's Fairy Tales. (Hodder & Stoughton.) 1913, reissued 1917, 1923.

The Works of Rabelais. (Navarre Society.) 1913.

A Midsummer Night's Dream, by William Shakespeare. (Constable.) 1914.

The Water Babies, by Charles Kingsley. (Constable.) 1915.

Some Frightful War Pictures. (Duckworth.) 1915.

Hunlikely. (Duckworth.) 1916.

Peacock Pie, by Walter de la Mare. (Constable.) 1916.

The Saintly Hun. (Duckworth.) 1917.

Get On With It. (Robinson & Birch.) 1920.

The Homemade Car, by W. Heath Robinson. (Duckworth.) 1921.

Old Time Stories, by Perrault. (Constable.) 1921.

Fly Papers. (Duckworth.) 1921.

Peter Quip in Search of a Friend. (Partridge.) 1922.

Quaint and Selected Pictures. (Robinson & Birch.) 1922.

Humours of Golf, by W. Heath Robinson. (Methuen.) 1923.

Topsy-Turvy Tales, by Elsie S. Munro. (John Lane, The Bodley Head.) 1923.

The Incredible Adventures of Professor Branestawm, by Norman Hunter. (John Lane, The Bodley Head.) 1933.

Absurdities. (Hutchinson.) 1934.

Heath Robinson's Book of Goblins, from Vernaleken's *In the Land of Marvels.* (Hutchinson.) 1934.

How to Live in a Flat, by K. R. G. Browne and Heath Robinson. (Hutchinson.) 1936.

How to be a Perfect Husband, by K. R. G. Browne and Heath Robinson. (Hutchinson.) 1937.

How to Make a Garden Grow, by K. R. G. Browne and Heath Robinson. (Hutchinson.) 1938.

How to be a Motorist, by K. R. G. Browne and Heath Robinson. (Hutchinson.) 1938.

Success with Stocks and Shares, by John B. Gledhill and Frank Preston. (Pitman.) 1938.

Let's Laugh. (Hutchinson.) 1939.

How to Make the Best of Things, by H. Cecil Hunt and Heath Robinson. (Hutchinson.) 1940.

Mein Rant, by Richard F. Patterson. (Blackie.) 1940.

Heath Robinson at War. (Methuen.) 1942.

How to Run a Communal Home, by H. Cecil Hunt and Heath Robinson. (Hutchinson.) 1943.

Once Upon a Time, by Liliane Clopet. (Müller.) 1944.